On the eve of ar

the ink of my mind is drenched with ...

mpT
MODERN POETRY IN TRANSLATION
The best of world poetry

No. 1 2020
© *Modern Poetry in Translation* 2019 and contributors

ISSN (print) 0969-3572
ISSN (online) 2052-3017
ISBN (print) 978-1-910485-26-2

Editor: Clare Pollard
Managing Editor: Sarah Hesketh
Digital Content Editor: Ed Cottrell
Finance Manager: Deborah De Kock
Design by Jenny Flynn
Cover art by Yoshino Shigihara
Typesetting by Libanus Press

Printed and bound in Great Britain by Charlesworth Press, Wakefield
For submissions and subscriptions please visit
www.modernpoetryintranslation.com

Modern Poetry in Translation Limited. A Company Limited by Guarantee
Registered in England and Wales, Number 5881603
UK Registered Charity Number 1118223

Modern Poetry in Translation gratefully acknowledges the support of
The Japan Society and The Great Britain Sasakawa Foundation

Translations of Chus Pato by Erin Moure
in this issue were supported by
the Translation Exchange at
Queen's College Oxford

Dream Colours

CONTENTS

Focus

Reviews

Like many readers around the world, I have always been attracted to Japanese culture. Whilst my son pores over Pokémon comics, I glance up at my bookshelves in the next room and can see novels by Murakami, Kawabata, Yoshimoto. Two of my favourite novels of the last year were Sayaka Murata's *Convenience Store Woman*, translated by Ginny Tapley Takemori, and Yōko Ogawa's *The Memory Police*, translated by Stephen Snyder.

And of course, as a poet, how could I not love the haiku? It is perhaps the most beloved form in the world, for its technical precision and brevity; its seasonal feeling; its ability to capture a moment like a photograph or, as Masaoka Shiki called it, a form of 'verbal sketching'. Basho memorably asked: 'Is there any good in saying everything?' and the idea of poetry as 'the half-said thing' is one of the most influential in the artform's history. Robert Hass' *The Essential Haiku: Versions of Basho, Buson and Issa* (Bloodaxe, 2013) is one of my most beloved books, pressed into the hands of my students, its images imprinted in my memory. I have often repeated Issa's haiku to arachnids:

> Don't worry, spiders,
> I keep house
> casually

The first winter rain always makes me think of Basho's monkey who 'seems to want a raincoat'; the Spring of his cherry blossoms falling 'in the salads, the soup, everywhere.'

Embarrassingly though, when I began my editorship at *Modern Poetry in Translation* I realised I knew almost nothing about contemporary Japanese poetry, so decided this was something I needed to remedy with a Japanese focus. My research began when I came across an article on Chika Sagawa, Japan's first female Modernist poet, who died of stomach cancer in 1936 at the age of only 24. I was absolutely blown away by her *Collected Poems*, translated by Sawako Nakayasu (Canarium Books, 2015), which feel both precise and disorientating, with their astonishing opening lines: 'Insects multiplied with the speed of an electric current'; 'Seasons change their gloves'; 'In the morning I see several friends escaping from the window'; 'Dreams are severed fruit'; 'With all of my ears | I listen'; 'Night eats colour'. Sawako Nakayasu is, I have since discovered, also a thrilling poet in her own right, experimenting with translations and 'anti-translations', who I am very pleased to include in this issue.

My education continued when Vahni Capildeo kindly brought a book back from Australia for us, the landmark anthology *Poet to Poet: Contemporary Women Poets from Japan*, edited by Rina Kikuchi and Jen Crawford (Recent Work Press, 2018), which Jennifer Lee Tsai reviewed in these pages, and which introduced me to poets such as the extraordinary Hiromi Ito, whose *Killing Kanoko/Wild Grass on the Riverbank* has just been published by Tilted Axis Press, translated by Jeffrey Angles. Since then we have been given advice and help by Junko Takekawa at Japan Foundation and translators like Andrew Houwen and Polly Barton, as well as support from the Japan Society and The Great Britain Sasakawa Foundation. Many thanks too, of course, to all in the translation community who submitted poems to this issue.

So I am very pleased to share with you in these pages a glimpse of some of the very exciting poetry happening in Japan beyond the haiku – a starting point, I hope, for further explorations (both for our readers and myself). In this Olympic year, as the eyes of the world are on Japan, we hope its poets will also gain some of the wider visibility they deserve.

Clare Pollard

SHLOMO LAUFER

Translated by Betsy Rosenberg

Shlomo Laufer is a prolific Hebrew poet and novelist, editor and translator. Born in war-torn Lvov in 1940, Laufer arrived in Israel with his family after a childhood of wandering. In 'Shutting Down' Laufer sings out the bewilderment of his early years with agonised hilarity. Both in prose and poetry, his irrepressible voice belies memories of displacement with a startling self-assurance gained perhaps through imagined encounters and fluid interchanges of identity with figures like Kafka, Chekhov, and Bruno Shultz. Laufer's style is insouciant and endearingly unsentimental, yet it resonates with undertones and overtones of violent longing.

Shutting Down

I shut the window, then the closet and the door,
the blinds where a moth
slipped through, I shut the doghouse,
the mouse hole.

The old train station
where a mist is rising,
the mound of a mole,
a bird's nest,
the hollow of a tree
shut down.

I shut the inkwell,
the poem spilling out of it.
I shut the dictionary and the word
'Hope' in my empty stomach.

I shut the mother-of-pearl,
the eyes, the tears, a small valise
of memories. I shut
museums,
pharmacies,
the harlots' stalls.

I shut Josef K. in the castle halls,
Freud in the asylum, Van Gogh's
sunflowers, the wound in the scab,
the water in the well, in the maw of
death, volcanoes deep in the earth,
my teeth in a broken jaw.

I shut my childhood in a little
urn of ashes. I shut a furrow in the soil
with marble and stone. I shut Plato in the cave,
I shut Europe, I shut God
between the covers of an empty book.
I shut my passions in a mouldy
cellar, my love in the irons of despair.
Shut up, shut up, I shout between sealed lips,
but it all stays open.

Translated by Kit Fan

Appearing in June 2019 at the beginning of mass protests in Hong Kong against the Anti-Extradition Law Amendment Bill, Bei Dao's 'June' captures the uncanny mood of a city in flux as the wind changes its direction seasonally and politically in 2019 in Hong Kong, as well as 30 years ago in Beijing. Summoning the invisible atmospheric force, the poem speaks, as if through a reported or borrowed speech from the wind, in an unashamedly direct tone akin to legal or political diction. However, line by line the directness is interrupted by flashes of emblematic images that evoke an urban cityscape in crisis ('the great concrete square', 'the left bank | of the dead'). The poem connects time, geography, and the act of writing and flight in an unpredictably palpable way, forging a high-pitched counter-balance between the questions of nationhood ('a flag'), fluidity ('the sea'), and coverage ('bass speakers') in a particular month of the year burdened with memory.

June

after Bei Dao

Wind is mouthing something in my mortised ear:
June

June stays blacklisted
while I hasten my disappearance

Please attend to the method of bidding
farewell

the audible respiration attached
to big words

Please attend to the interpretations of not-us:
plastic flowers blooming like umbrellas

on the open horizon or the left bank
of the dead

The great concrete square is extended
through writing

as in this moment
where my written characters take flight

where dawn is forged somewhere else
and a flag shrouds the sea

as ocean and her faithful bass speakers announce
June

Introduced by Chris Beckett
Translated by Yemisrach Tassew and Chris Beckett

I was in Addis Ababa last July to try and finish off the anthology of
Amharic poetry in English – the first such anthology ever! – which I
have been working on with Alemu Tebeje and other friends like
Yemisrach Tassew for the last few years. It is being published by
Carcanet in May 2020. One of my main aims was to track down a few
more women poets, since it is still the case that Ethiopian men rush
to print much quicker than women! Misrak was recommended to me
by the president of the Ethiopian Writers Association, and I went off
to meet her and her friend Mihret Kebede, another wonderful young
woman poet, at the old Ras Hotel where they were preparing for a big
jazz and poetry event, in a series they started and still organise every
month. Misrak is soft spoken, but as I had been told, she is also
fearless. She writes about unpleasant acts, such as the appalling rape
and murder of a baby girl, and unpleasant situations such as being
dumped by your lover, but there is no sentimentality, rather a
forensic eye for the freshest words, rhythm, image to express such
basic experiences in a poem. The results are often surprisingly lyrical
and moving.

What Did You Find So Beautiful?

for a one-year old baby girl, raped and killed

My feet had not begun to walk,
    my mouth to speak,
I was no earthly good at laughing,

even so...
my eyes could not see clearly what they saw,
my hands were still too soft to fight,
but even so...
I was still a crawler on the ground,
a creature making words which only I could catch,
so how could you have won
    by beating me?
how was my loss your victory?
    my girl your man?
was it my babyhood that made you brave?
please tell me, what was it in the end
which tempted you into my little bed?
what did you find so beautiful?
my hips, my chest, my long hair or my legs?
my scent of pee or sweat?
I could call you Killer, Rapist, you who married me
    to earth...
but oh please, tell me on my life,
what did you find so beautiful?

Please Come for Me!

My body knows that spring is here,
the thunder in my ears,
my skin on tenterhooks,
my heart that breathes again...
all my senses start to fight,
split down the middle,

my eyes go separate ways,
left wells up missing you,
right searching you in crowds...
my nose splinters,
one nostril sniffs for you,
the other puffs out smoke from a cigarette...
body-signs announcing spring,
my feet itch and my heart beats faster,
my ears hear separate bells,
one pricks up at your step,
the other plays a memory chip...
even my hands that greeted you
forget they are a pair,
one waves goodbye,
the other thinks you may be coming back...
one leg rushes off to town,
the other only wants to follow you
or wait in case you pass by on the street.
But now perhaps the time has come?
my eyelids flutter, shoulders shiver,
my heart beats in my mouth,
oh! come, please come and stitch
my senses back together,
bring this too-long waiting to an end,
come quick as quick you can,
come for me now, come back forever!

DURS GRÜNBEIN

Translated by Karen Leeder

These four cantos come from Durs Grünbein's *Porzellan: Poem vom Untergang meiner Stadt* (Porcelain: Poem on the Downfall of My City) of 2005. This is a book length cycle consisting of forty-nine ten-line poems written over a decade that explore the poet's hometown of Dresden through the prism of the Allied firebombing in February 1945 (seventy-five years ago this year). The poem operates on multiple levels, moving back to the founding of Dresden as the famed 'Venice on the Elbe', through the war years, and especially the bombing itself, through Grünbein's childhood in East Germany, and ending with the rebuilding of Dresden's famous Frauenkirche in 2004. The image of Meissen porcelain – Dresden's 'white gold' – both holds the cycle together but also suggests the multiple fractures of history. The poem is haunted by these various pasts and by the many literatures which have preceded it, as suggested by the title, which holds within it the covert dedication ('por Celan') for the great Holocaust poet. The poem is rhymed and moves in and out of classical meter, shifting between high poetic diction, irony, humour and the downright demotic, concerned always with the poet's role as a keeper and creator of memories, 'changing places, times, dimensions as he goes – goes on – creating' (canto 49). Controversially, perhaps, the poem sets itself against what Grünbein calls the 'myth' of the Germans as innocent victims of an exceptional and unjustified act of war carried out by the notorious Sir Arthur Bomber Harris, on Churchill's orders; setting out instead the background to the air-war Germany itself unleashed. But it never loses sight of the horror deliberately visited on an unwitting civilian population, nor the devastation which looms so large in the German memory.

13

And if any mischief follow, then
thou shalt give ... burning for burning,
Exodus 21

No sweat, Arthur, you only did what you had to do.
A duel requires a steady hand, nerves of steel, it's true,
though *Blitzkrieg* is more Moses: an 'eye for an eye' kind of deal.
You knew your Bible back to front, had an iron will,
got 'em though, the Huns, Nibelungs – and Antichrists, why not.
No need to tell an Englishman about what's fair.
'Acts of terror'? Memo. Your canny Prime Minister –
washed his hands of it, like Pilate. Whiter than white,
he's gone down in history. Now the fat is in the fire:
Terror-Merchant, Bingo-Bomber, Desk-Pirate of the Skies.

14

Still not done? How's about the seventeenth of April?
Alarms wake those still wandering the ruins, the bereaved.
Spring, a shadow of life. Out of nowhere, into the still
of the graveyard, bursts a squadron of killer bees.
Flying Fortress is the scourge and it takes its time.
All quiet below, apathy, no flak-guns thunder.
Forests, motorways – just a field of rubble. 'Alright!'
And just like that the world we knew went under,
Dresden now was just a patch of prairie land.
....
One come from the future, *ex machina*, forgive the man.

After the completed renovation
of the Frauenkirche, 23 June 2004

Then and now ... our memory a pendulum,
always swinging back and forth. Tread carefully, though
it will curtail your little span and, slowing, take its toll.
You're impressed, though, when you hear how she would fall
only later, when the night of bombs had passed,
Frauenkirche, true lady that she is, gave her children
time to heal. Sorely wounded, she held out to the last,
standing proud, despite her broken spine.
After and before. ... Her subsidence the caesura.
Through all those years, the lesson was: stay upright just like her.

Luther standing there: the image I can't let go.
Surrounded by a wasteland, shoots of tender green,
under a disdainful sky, almost forgotten, a *memento*
of the blaze: and in this urban desert, a window arch remains.
Do you recall? The lonely risalit, black with soot,
moaning soundlessly, like the 'o' in torso ... chorus ... baroque.
A mote like this in your eye and you're stuck
with it for life. And yet the greatest shock
was not the ruined church, his final thesis –
but that all around the sheep grazed on oblivious.

CHUS PATO

Translated by Erín Moure

Un Libre Favor hails the possibility of poetry and language in our lives. Pato's title literally says 'A Free Favour,' echoing Kant on aesthetics (*Critique of Judgment*, 1790). The exercise of holding something in favour is, to Kant, freedom.

In Galician, *favor* is a gift bestowed without hope of return. *Libre* means 'free'; *de balde* or *gratuíto* mean 'free of charge.' In our English 'free,' the mercantile echoes of 'free of charge' overpower the idea of freedom and of freely holding in favour. And our 'favour' leaves the impression of something not quite freely given, that expects a return. Other English translations of Kant squirm: 'a free favour', a free favouring, a free favour, a *free favour*, an unconstrained favouring. All too awkward! Yet any move away from these translations tends to lose Kant, or introduce unwanted meanings. Best to leap sideways, thus: *The Face of the Quartzes.*

Here, Pato explores our relations as *sapiens* with the natural, with the natal, with impropriety (for life cannot be property), and with language itself, in an era that seems close to a planetary end-time. The poems, though dark, are firmly celebratory.

In Neolithic times, the *Gallaeci*, Chus Pato's ancestors, would insert white quartzes at intervals in the east face of a megolithic tomb. Facing dawn, this wall marks the portal between the worlds of the living and the dead. Through it, when the light of dawn dazzles the quartzes, you can pass between the worlds.

Poetry too is such a portal.

Five Poems from Un Libre Favor |
The Face of the Quartzes

THE HAND assembles words
my hand
that misjudges the size of the letters and width of the wall
Up above
a bullet penetrates the cry
separates the letters
the syllables
bodies tumble from the peak
The hand returns beside the others
all of them archaic
red black ochre
they agitate
like a handkerchief waving goodbye
They sleep underfoot
heads downward
like bats

BRISA fills her apron
with flowers,
sprung from an island's umbilicus;
when the Prelude cuts a narcissus
the earth opens, and the coursers carry her away
via the very volcano in which Empedocles vanished
the dogs lose the scent and muddle the hunt
the pigs are led to the abyss
Her companion is one of time's childrren

she savours one, two, three seeds
of pomegranate
If I go mute it's not to keep a secret
it's only an initiation
a start.
The dear girl is unspeakable
it's autumn
it's spring
and in serene nights of summer
atop a garden wall she cries out
aletheia, aletheia!
You wanted fire to come through the windows
or ice
that they shatter
that the dust be cleared off the toys;
fantasy trembles like the golds in the aspen
don't cry, mother, on the stones of Eleusis
the emerald is now liquid
I'll spring into your eyes

SO IT'S NOT THE GIRL who eyes death
but Hades who admires the girl
in whom is imprinted all the beauty of the world?
Would you recognize god,
would you speak of him as you did of your brother
he has the shapeliest legs in the cosmos
and his arms can embrace every land,
when you surrendered and sat on slabs of marble
in your faint?

Time is tight, yes, but it's also what
a person grants to herself and grants to others
and concedes to god
It's dark-ochre and red,
the face of the lover

traced in blood

WHAT WAS I SAYING TO you
that I preferred watching the Solomonic columns
carts that crossed the bridge carrying the gold to Rome?
I had a job on that bridge
mandated by poverty
Yes, I was the girl who vanished
and came in the door talking of dogs
and who tarried under the huge advert for timepieces
who was lost in tunnels that opened onto a river
You're not taking care
I know how to carve buffalo that turn their heads backward
and are projected into the splendour
That's understanding,
a jackal that traces its way in the night
and judges
The sky
we discern it
by the glaucous
ridge
that the snow didn't quite hide

Skylark
turn your trill to me
child of lightning that I am
sew me up with its glinting needle
sing me
along with the horses

Those of us
from the woodlands and the knights-errant
it's been awhile
since we existed
but the high grass of May
– blackbirds plunge into it –
and the wandering amazons
fall down
breaking free of the book

you pat snow into another snowball
we hold onto the halter rope
and the exhausted knight

to those men and women
amiable
who sport stockings the colour of meadows with floating butterflies
hair rebelling against straighteners and dye
and the purse stuck to its flower

if you mix sunlight with the bones
and infiltrate granite

you might able to write a country
perhaps amazon and knight might awaken from their trance
and return to the pages,
a country opens up at some point along the way

when I say 'that force is nature'
I say 'sapiens language is nature'

that is the meditation

BENJAMIN FONDANE

Translated by Clarissa Aykroyd

Benjamin Fondane (1898–1944) was a man who lived across borders. He grew up in Romania, produced most of his mature philosophy, poetry and other work in France, and went as far afield as Argentina to work on the now-lost film *Tararira*. He was also Jewish, an identity which he explored extensively in his poems, and which made him a target. Fondane died in a concentration camp in 1944, but his poetry survives and distills an extraordinary life. His longer works such as *Ulysses* (1933) and *Titanic* (1937) return repeatedly to themes of wandering, displacement and exploration. Fondane's shorter lyric poems also feature such themes.

These two poems are among Fondane's final writings, collected after his death under the title of *Au temps du poème* (In the Time of the Poem). French was not Fondane's first language, and perhaps this contributes to the highly distinctive nature of his voice. He is wry, tragic, imagistic, measured, passionate, very often in the space of just a few lines. A translator of Fondane just needs to listen carefully and let him speak without interference.

All at Once

I was in the middle
of reading a book
when all at once
I saw my window
fill up its absent eye with airy drunken birds.

Yes, it was snowing.
Snowing like mad!
It fell
peaceful and light
in a heart full of holes like a fishing net.

It was so good!
and I was drunk
on those flakes
so happy to be alive
that my forgetful hand let the book fall!

How I saw
the snow coming down
in a naked heart!
Oh God! If only
I'd known to keep in my heart a bit of that snow!

Still in the middle
of reading a book!
Still in the middle
of writing a book!
And all at once the peaceful snow in my window!

When the Shipwrecked Traveller

When the shipwrecked traveller
came at last to the island, having saved
his toothbrush, pipe, liver trouble and
an old disbelief in miracles from the waves,
time dissolved suddenly like the snow pack,
silence suddenly crackled everywhere,
the traveller's blood became light and drunk
so drunk and so light
that he went into things and things went
into him in an incandescent thirst so vivid
that his sight stumbled amongst visions,
suffered vertigo, such strong hallucinations,
ecstasies and revelations
so clear, that he became afraid of himself, of becoming
a spider, or a wild strawberry –
so afraid that he threw himself to his knees, praying
to his god who was too great to do miracles,
and let himself fall from a cliff into the sea
just an instant before
he would have received the gift of prophecy.

LAURA FUSCO

Translated by Caroline Maldonado

Laura Fusco's writing is impelled by her commitment to human rights and is expressed through performance of various kinds, often in collaboration with musicians and dancers. She sees herself writing and performing in the tradition of the bard who gives voice to the unheard. These three poems are taken from a forthcoming collection, *Liminal*, to be published in English translation from the original Italian in April 2020 by Smokestack Books. It is a scrapbook of stories, graffiti and placards, songs of exile and songs against exile, a book about learning to live outside and between borders, stateless and homeless, invisible and unheard, marginal. In it Laura Fusco records the voices of refugees arriving in Europe, particularly through the Mediterranean via Italy and France, from Syria, Iraq, Afghanistan and other countries from which they are forcibly displaced. She especially seeks out the voices of women she has met in camps along the way.

When I read the original version of *Limbo* I was struck by the intimacy and urgency of the many voices which work together almost as one immense chorus. The accretion of voices and physical details from the refugees' environment give the reader a sense of everything being close and in the present and yet part of a terrible and universal odyssey.

Fusco's lines are open and sometimes barely punctuated, seemingly without end, mirroring the endless migratory movement of their subject matter, and at some points they become fragmentary, separated by gaps. I aimed to catch their tone, rhythm and breath, when necessary searching for equivalencies of sound in English. Only when I'd read the texts aloud again and again could I judge whether they approached the effect of the original.

Lo Sgombero, tu Sgomberi*

Electricity off,
candles burnt out,
on the sideboard rice grains
stuck to the saucepan's base.
You wake up,
hair still knotted to the dream clouds of half an hour ago,
tiny dancer's breasts underneath a frenzy
of hair,
you haven't been here long,
in the midst of life's chaos you're learning words,
here there's nothing else to do and even if it's late
someone starts to play music and doesn't stop.
Fields
which will flower with poppies
move along in a sequence of stills.
Sounds belonging to day enter night.
Is that an instruction
to go over there?
In the river bed
there was water and now there's fire. Each word
like a spark
burns.
Io sgombero, tu sgomberi.
The volunteer teaches Italian.
Someone switches channels on her iphone,
searching for the hero from her favourite soap.
By 8 o'clock the night's fluorescent and full of stars.

*I evict, you evict

Eviction

The Jungle:
plastic tents, wooden prefabs,
communal kitchens, distribution sites for clothes, outlets for Eritrean food,
has been surrounded
at dawn.
Stones fly,
then fly no more.
Iraqis, Afghanis, Syrians, Lebanese, Sudanese, Pakistanis.
Someone tries to escape between the armoured cars.
After the eviction the destruction starts,
a sock's left behind,
heaps of plastic and blankets,
a kettle whistles into the emptiness,
a doll on a branch watches the tea
boil over.

Mais C'est Quoi?

Clouds race.
Sun gleams on the cars
and the wall lengthens to support the lizard fleeing
from the hand of the boy who's dreaming he'll be the one to drive them
far away.
Every night his father reaches the dream with empty hands.
He no longer has a mother.
Like the tides
now high, now low,
with a life to start over again. First
the eviction from the squat at La Chapelle
then the occupied school Jean Quarré
and Austerlitz
and Saint Ouen.
Mais c'est quoi?
Metro Stalingrad, Parigi, Paris, Péris.
After the thunder and hailstones he steps out of a rainbow with a
biscuit.
What will be, will be. Like all the others
he'll line up his French days to rewrite his language,
they'll either let him do it or not.
Life's not paradise.
But if you step out of a rainbow most of it's done,
maybe....
Then he starts to run.

EFE DUYAN

Translated by Tara Skurtu and Efe Duyan

If poetry is, like an asymptote, language constantly approaching a
given feeling but never quite meeting it at any finite distance, then
Turkish poet Efe Duyan's poetry captures both the asymptote and the
curve which resists this approach: language is at a loss. It literally
disappears, and describes its own disappearance. How to describe an
action when you're in the wake of losing the verb? Efe translates the
silent intention behind our instinctive, urgent need of human
expression and connection. Duyan's 'The Verbs of a Language are
Forgotten First' explores the silence of eroding substitution, and
translating this poem was quite a challenge in carrying over the
meaning of these vestigial parts of speech into the wordless space in
which love and fear remain. The trickiest yet most flexible part of
translating this poem was figuring out the word order and line breaks
– Turkish syntax differs from that of English so much that there is a
spectrum of options, and I tried to place the puzzle pieces of phrases
in an English that maintains as much of the tone, voice, and feeling
of this poem in which language itself erodes, in time and in love, into
complete silence.

The Verbs of a Language are Forgotten First

first we forget the verbs
they fall away
leaving behind
a small wave

then the untranslatable
adjectives
we use carefully
for great pain

then the adverbs
from an ancient language
no longer spoken

then the absurd interjections
of our childhood
making us happy
out of nowhere

then the nouns darken
slow and flow
into the sea along
with the rainwater

only the fear of death remains

we don't speak anymore
but it keeps beating like a pulse
that nameless skill
permeating us as we wait
to call the words back

RAYMOND QUENEAU

Translated by Philip Terry

In 2017 I met the writer Lily Robert-Foley who, like me, was participating in a series of events organised by Jeff Hilson and Zöe Skoulding under the title *Expanded Translation*. We both had a longstanding interest in the work of Oulipo, the *Ouvroir de littérature potentielle* (or Workshop of Potential Literature). Lily, I soon discovered, was one of the founding members of Outranspo, one of the Ou-x-pos that have emerged from Oulipo to apply Oulipian ideas in different fields. Outranspo, in brief, put their energies not into inventing new formal constraints for writers to use – the work of Oulipo – but into inventing new modes of translation for the translator to explore. *Multitranslation*, for example, describes a translation that simultaneously offers multiple translations for the same word, foregrounding the fact that every translation makes choices, and that these choices could always be made differently. It reminds us that translation never operates on a 1:1 correspondence across languages.

As soon as Lily introduced me to their ideas I was hooked. At the time I'd just started to translate Raymond Queneau's *Exercises de style*, and I saw at once that it could be interesting to translate Queneau's story about a petty argument on a bus using the methods of Outranspo. Queneau himself wrote far more than the ninety-nine variations he published in book form, and this would be a way of further multiplying and unfolding Queneau's narrative, one of the founding texts of Oulipo. It seemed irresistible.

I soon started to freely invent my own methods. Some of the results made their way into *The Penguin Book of Oulipo*, which I was editing at the time, a selection of the others is reproduced below. 'Ryanair' and 'Ice Age' are free inventions, 'Homomovocalism' and 'Lemon Tree Howl' pick up on ideas from Oulipo and Outranspo, the latter a homophonic translation from Queneau's French, where sound rather than sense is translated. 'Hidden English' borrows an idea from poet Peter Manson in his book *English in Mallarmé* (2014), where he extracts English words hidden in Mallarmé's French.

Neutral

In the S bus, in the rush hour. A bloke about 26, felt hat with a cord instead of a ribbon, neck too long as if someone had been tugging at it. People getting off. The bloke in question gets annoyed with one of the men standing next to him. He accuses him of bumping into him every time someone goes past. A whining tone which is meant to sound menacing. When he sees a vacant seat, he grabs it.

Two hours later, I come across him in Cour de Rome, in front of the Gare Saint-Lazare. He's with a friend who's saying: 'You should get another button put on your overcoat.' He shows him where (at the lapels) and why.

Ice Age

Beneath the shelter of the mouth of the cave, in the rain. A hunter, in his early manhood, hair in a man-bun with twigs stuck in it instead of feathers. People of the tribe drift into the cave. The hunter gets annoyed with one of the old men standing next to him, grunts at him, accusing him of shoving him every time someone pushes past to enter the cave. A whistling tone which is meant to sound threatening. When the rain stops he goes off.

Later, when the sun has gone down, I see him sitting round the fire in the camp. He is with the shaman who's saying: 'You should get rid of those twigs in your hair.' He takes one out and throws it in the fire to show him why.

Ryanair

In seat 5B, just after boarding. A bloke about 26, party hat with a turntable instead of a brim, bag too elongated as if it contained a six person tent. People pushing to get into their seats. The bloke in question gets annoyed with one of the men standing next to him. He accuses him of bumping into him every time he tries to hoist his bag into the overhead lockers. A whining tone which is meant to sound menacing. When he sees a vacant seat, he puts his bag there.

Three hours later, I come across him in Tenerife, in front of the Bureau de Change. He's with a friend who's saying: 'You should get another zip put on your carpet bag.' He shows him where (the seam is split at one end) and why (there's the nose of a sausage dog poking out).

Homovocalism

In the sun, six ex-cub scouts. Another day out, eating anchovies, salmon, sprats, brill, oysters. Too hot, says Bill. Someone sends a text, spews up in a bin. George, then Ian, open some tins. Wunderkid Don gets annoyed with one of the Bens arsing next to him. He accuses him of burping. Ionides tells Ben in text to fetch some roes and a brill in for Meiki, deaf to Don's surreal snipe. He sees a vacant seal, beats it.

Two hours later, I come across Bill in Flounders Hoe, in front of the ape park, in a rage. He sings shanties of Bali: 'Ou-ou-e-aoe-uo-u-o-ou-oeoa-eo-i-ee-a e-ae-a!'

Hidden English

after Peter Manson

```
    an      he    affluence  type
       in  six  a  chap          cordon
    cant   ban     long      on
       tire          dent    type
    question   rite con      sin
                     pass
    Ton     chard          chant  me
      it    place lib             us


    he    plus tar     con    our
    Rome  ant  are Saint     are
      rad     it      is fair
      bout    ent     ton par
      on              pour
```

Lemon Tree Howl

danceless honoured
affluence
untype 'danceless'
hover in guts
six hands
cheap or mauve
rump lacing
the rub
and cut rope
long commission
only await
tired jesus
legends descend
let hype
in questions
err rite
constrain vision
Ill we reproach
deli bus
colour check
forest kill
pass skeleton
tone pillar
niche hard
keys savour
merchant come
heel vote
a palace library
see precipitates

suss dues
hours plus
tar gel
wrong country
coward roamed
event lag
a recent laser
less to have
a con camarade
keel ditto
devours farm
utter 'unbutton'
supplement tear
a tone pard
eases a lemon
tree howl
a chant crude
head pour
ark
u.o.i.

VOLHA HAPEYEVA

Translated by Annie Rutherford

'The Heart Regenerates' was one of the first poems of Volha Hapeyeva's that I read, and it convinced me that I wanted to translate this poet. The poem is characteristic for Volha's work, which typically combines a surreal vision with explorations of the body, memory and social and gendered injustices. Full of intentional gaps and daring leaps in meaning, these explanations pose a number of satisfying challenges to the translator. In 'The Heart Regenerates', these gaps come from Volha's application of anatomical research to our typically figurative understanding of the heart. In doing so, she manages to write about love without sentimentality and memory without nostalgia.

Since that first reading, I've been working with Volha for around eighteen months. Our paths first crossed, fittingly enough, through translation – we translate the same German poet, Nora Gomringer, into our respective languages. Aware that I speak Russian, Volha approached me about a potential translation collaboration to bring her work into English; translators from Belarusian into English are few and far between, and Belarusian and Russian are closely related (similar to, say, Spanish and Portuguese), offering me a shortcut into accessing the language.

Belarusian is sometimes considered an endangered language, with fewer active users of the language than the population of Scotland. As is the case with many endangered or minority languages, the decision to write in Belarusian (rather than Russian) is highly charged, one which is both personal and political.

The Heart Regenerates

the heart regenerates
more slowly than other organs
and is never renewed
completely
that's what it says in the textbook

this means
I think
that everyone in there will remain

the left side of one person's body will be erased
a face will disappear
a new one growing in the place of the old
languages, years, names
will intermingle

in my garden of mutants
where we lost our way

When a Tree Dies

when a tree dies
pink nipples
bow their heads
as a sign of mourning

when a tree dies
it grows dark
as all eyes hide their shame
behind eyelash curtains

when a tree dies
I console
my lover's pain
with medicinal lips
I bandage their body
with fingers and hands

when a tree dies
someone takes my head between their palms
in silence
and falls asleep
while somewhere beyond the window
my tree is dying

ALEŠ ŠTEGER

Translated by Brian Henry

Over the past 25 years, Aleš Šteger's poems have taken on various
forms and modes – free verse, prose poems, first-person lyric narra-
tives, meditations on single words, object poems. One constant,
though, is the philosophical thread that runs through all of his work.
The two poems by Šteger in this issue – 'Mountain' and 'Syracuse' –
are among a group of poems written since he published his most
recent book, *Above the Sky Beneath the Earth*, in Slovenia in 2015. Many
of his newer poems have a song-like quality, complete with refrains
and, sometimes, words that sound more than mean; a few of the
poems inhabit or mimic traditional forms such as the sonnet and
haiku. The effect is partly classical, but, given the allusions to
contemporary crises – here, environmental destruction and the
Syrian refugee crisis – also disorienting and provocative. Whether he
examines the 'architecture of pain' or a mountain, he 'persistently
evades' the expected, juxtaposing the past and the present with
startling precision.

Syracuse

Spellbound by histories.
Athena and the Virgin in one.
The architecture of pain
And the cries of gulls over the shore.

The eye is impartially hungry
For stucco, cherubim, Doric wars,
Ecstatically in time,
Which shields it from the present.

It's a pleasure pleasure pleasure
To stroll around Syracuse
Because once it was Aleppo.

On the screens, rafts. In the water, bodies.
I blindly stare at indifferent stones.
The past is now and here since long ago.

Mountain

This mountain does and does not have a name.
It has a name that persistently evades.

Not a name, only a mute crease
Of yet another everyday loss.

In vain you address the clearing of pines,
In vain the black stomachs of clouds.

The name of the mountain persistently evades,
Teaches you, without purpose, without cause,

To seek, to call, to shout,
To despair, to toy with despair.

Mountain mountain mountain in front of me.
Scree scree scree inside.

Inside, where there are many broken shadows,
A lot of scree but no trees.

From the scree a silent rock grows.
From the silent rock, a solid mountain.

This mountain does and does not have a name.
It has a name that persistently evades.

A mountain mountain mountain in me.
Scree scree scree everywhere.

AXEL SCHULZE

Translated by Steph Morris

Translating the 1960s diaries of East German novelist Brigitte Reimann sucked me into GDR literary life. She describes how in 1969, along with various novels, the anthology *Saison für Lyrik* (Aufbau, 1968) was criticized for negativity and individualism. A showcase anthology, it includes today's GDR grandees (Reiner Kunze, Elke Erb, Volker Braun etc.) and one Axel Schulze, poems with strong images, physicality and a sense of the poet's presence as active observer. Little information is accessible on him. He published several collections in the 1970s and 1980s in the GDR, all out of print. This poem appeared later in a revised form, the version translated here, in the anthology *Lyrik der DDR* (Aufbau 1979) and in his first collection, *Zu ebener Erde* (Mitteldeutscher Verlag, 1973). That book's design is refreshingly inventive, square, illustrated, and laid out with the poems' stanzas and titles in surprising places on the page, like an art book or a magazine. This poem's numbered stanzas zig-zag across two pages, enhancing the sense these are discrete observations placed alongside gaps, a sense of some things said, others not. I haven't reproduced this layout as it seems particular to that book, its designer having effectively collaborated with the poet; in *Lyrik der DDR* it becomes rectilinear again.

Many East German writers accepted the state's challenge for artists to engage with workers. They were placed in factories, joined brigades and shadowed construction workers. This feels like the product of one such scheme – a poetic, particular response.

The Tracklayers

1

hardened tracks cut through basalt
rust rubs off on their legs

2

this is about the sweat under their arms
about the tin flasks they drink from, water
at midday, where the sun crackles like foil
and they retreat to the shade of the tool truck

3

the table is wet with beer
here they bend their dripping necks
here they break their bread at rest

4

they may yet sleep on the quarry floor
they may yet snap off a dusty flower

5

their days in the stewed, sulphurous light
tough days, which burn the shoulders
and tear hot skin from the hands
tough days, when pebbles fly up
and the night fills the sky in a bloodburst

6

the engine's whistle splits their hours
breath shifts their damaged lungs
they raise the pickaxe through sweat and ash

7

I saw their shirts
I ate their sharp soup
I waited with them for rain

8

in the morning they run fresh water
over their faces and still
sense last night's sleep
as they unwrap coarse-grained bread
from the paper pack
their hands are heavy at night

9

they walk home in the dust
a potato flower in a buttonhole
an iris in a cup

HASAN ALIZADEH

Translated by Rebecca Ruth Gould and Kayvan Tahmasebian

The modernist poet and short story writer Hasan Alizadeh (b. 1947, Mashhad, Iran) has left a poetic signature on Persian poetry through his two volumes of poetry: *Rūznama-yi tabʿīd* (Diary of House Arrest), 2003, awarded the Karnameh Poetry Award, and *Ducharkha-yi ābī* (Blue Bicycle), 2015. *Diary of House Arrest* alludes in the title to the house arrest of Iranian Prime Minister Mohammad Mossadegh, following the US and British-led coup of 1953. *Blue Bicycle* is a collection of lyrical poems that engage with classical themes from Greco-Roman antiquity, European folklore, and Sufi mysticism.

In his poem, 'Mirror', Alizadeh indulges his fascination with mirrors as objects that reflect and refract alternate realities (see also 'Sleepwalking Mirror', 'Death', and 'Narcissus of Lovers', among the poems that we have translated). The poem recounts an encounter with death of the other (here of a young woman). The mirror serves a symbolic function in this poem. It refers to a mutual identification (as if between a person and their mirror image) –here between the poet and the young woman. The young woman becomes the poet by creating 'death from a cold woman's bones on the eighth day'; the poet becomes the woman who 'was brought | – I was bleeding – | to the hospital only to die.' Here as throughout Alizadeh's poetry, the motif of mirror is associated with death.

The magma-like dream world that Alizadeh evokes throughout his work, and the unpredictable juxtapositions of his poetics, together constitute the defining features of his voice within contemporary Iranian poetry. The poet's formalist lyricism posits poetry as an event that opens life onto the contingency of creaturely existence. Our translations seek to make manifest the clarity and precision of diction that characterizes Alizadeh's poetics.

Mirror

She was brought to hospital
to die –
she was bleeding.
'Won't survive,' the nurse said in cold blood & hard
as she drew down the seaweed-coloured scarf.

More beautiful than her anxious youth
with no blame, no shame,
she was passing away in my eyes –
she was bleeding.
She had been taken to hospital
as if to die.
It was the morning of February 8.
I was passing on the sunny pavement.

Beautiful,
pale,
silent,
she was passing away in my eyes.
She passed away.
She went
to the hospital as if only to die.

We wake up
with death masks
in newspapers
& staircases & streets.

You created death
from a cold woman's bones
on the eighth day.
No!
I'm not your mirror.
But I
was brought
– I was bleeding –
to the hospital only to die.

DREAM COLOURS

Focus on Japan

SAYAKA OSAKI

Translated by Jeffrey Angles

One day you wake up and realise how this world is already made so well and so stably. It makes you sad and angry and irritated at the same time, letting you know that there's almost nothing left that you can change or make anew. There is a Japanese culture called 'Origami', with which you can create almost anything from one square of colourful paper. 'Dazzled by the Morning Light...' is a poem using this motif – the hands hope to create their own world, struggling with so much noise surrounding them.

This poem was first published in the May 2007 issue of *Gendai Shitecho* magazine. Osaki appeared in the Japanese poetry world for the very first time with this poem before she started to focus more on listening to nature and animal voices after the Great East Japan Earthquake in 2011. The simple and easy manual work of folding various things with origami tamed her feeling of irritation caused by the vulnerability of self-existence.

Dazzled by the Morning Light...

The morning light was dreadfully dazzling
I folded some paper without thinking
Creating
A paper turtle, a paper swan, a paper squirrel,
A paper shrimp, a paper camel, a paper frilled lizard
The frilled lizard was level-five difficulty
First fold the paper in half
Fold to the centre along the dotted line
Fold to the centre against along the dotted line and open again

I fold and fold and fold and fold and fold and fold
Wanting to escape the dreadful light

I was always folding
Morning light poured through the window
My folding hands never stopped
I made a paper cicada
Made a paper crab
Made a paper balloon with rabbit ears
I folded a feeding trough for them
Folded a pail for them to drink
Folded a tree for the cicada to perch on
Folded a rock for the crab to hide beneath
Folded the air to make the balloon-rabbit bulge

My folding hands never stopped
Morning light poured through the window
I kept folding
Didn't care if my fingers peeled or bled
Didn't care if my nails cracked and shed
But my fingers didn't peel, my nails didn't crack
Never even bled
I didn't fold nearly enough for that

The sound of folding irritated my ears
I covered my ears
I tried to fold while covering my ears but failed
I had to make a choice:
Cover my ears or fold paper
I decided to fold
And started folding again

I put up with the irritating sound
Put up with it while folding a piano
Put up with it while folding a bed
Put up with it while folding a mug
The dazzling morning light grew soft
The sound of folding paper grew loud and echoed
I wanted to cover my ears but my hands were busy
I wanted somebody to cover these ears – anybody
I called out to whoever might be there
Anyone there? Anyone there? Anyone there?
I folded as I called out loud
Folded a shirt as I called out loud
Folded a skirt as I called out loud
Folded a child as I called out loud
I kept folding and folding and folding

And then
Someone's hands covered my ears
The sound of folding stopped
In an instant
I nodded off

There was no more sound of folding
Pleased, I kept on folding
My hands and ears covered up
My hands and ears were satisfied
I was relieved
The only problem
The morning light was dreadfully dazzling

SAWAKO NAKAYASU

with translations by Sawako Nakayasu, Lynn Xu and
Kyoko Yoshida

These poems are excerpted from *Some Girls Walk Into The Country
They Are From* (forthcoming, Wave Books, 2021). They were written
between 2017-2019, a period in which I returned to the US – 'the
country I am from' – after spending a significant amount of time in
Asia. The book collects poems and translations, and abandons
conventional notions distinguishing literary texts from their transla-
tions. In this 'non-binary' space, a translation might be partial,
multiple, incorrect, unfaithful, failed, 'anti-,' punk, or otherwise
capricious and errant. This continuum speaks to and from migration,
linguistic mechanisms of the brain, and multilingualism in a myriad
of embodiments.

The poem 'Sink or Swim' was translated by myself into Chinese
– for a performance called 'Asian White Feminist Performance,' first
performed at the Solomon R. Guggenheim Museum as part of
Glitch: An Evening of Poetry and Catalogue Launch for the exhibi-
tion, One Hand Clapping. It was subsequently edited together with
Lynn Xu. The Japanese translation was made entirely by Kyoko
Yoshida, and led to my writing an 'English-Japanese-English' transla-
tion, the first of this set of four.

Top: Sawako Nakayasu, bottom: Lynn Xu

Sink or Swim

Translation by Sawako Nakayasu via Kyoko Yoshida

When the pool spills over with bloody white wine, only Girl F, Girl H, and Girl I are willing to lend out another drowning. The grand sea of humanity churns and only Girl Detective knows the destination. Girl Investment claims she will come to the rescue as necessary but do you believe her. A puddle of hands disappears into the reflection of bonsai trees, Girl D thinks hard about the 'kiss of life,' decides firmly to scout out Girl F, F, F, indeed Girl F all over again.

Sink or Swim

Translation with Lynn Xu

水位上升时，汽车熄火, 只有 Girl F, Girl H, 和 Girl I能够帮忙.
人海中, Girl A常常在无名的路上讨饭 。突然Girl C救了她 。
一阵风吹来 。

最后路灯婚姻的光

　　　　　搞乱——擦汗

假装（换）丈夫 。

Sink or Swim

When the pool consists of water, only Girl F, Girl H, and Girl I are capable of lending a hand. In an ocean of people, it is Girl A who knows her way around and Girl C who will come to the rescue when you need it. In the fading light reflected off of a puddle of water, Girl D contemplates her 'life decisions' and determines to trade in her 'husband.'

_____か_____か

Translation by Kyoko Yoshida

プールが＿＿から成る場合、少女F、少女H、少女Iのみが＿＿を貸すことができる。＿＿の大海において、少女＿＿は行き先を知っており、少女＿＿は必要とあれば助けに来る。＿＿たまりに映る消えゆく＿＿の中で、少女＿＿は「人生の＿＿」について熟慮し「＿＿」を下取りに出す決心をする。

1. 北極熊	2. 沈む	3. C	4. 探偵	5. 水	6. E
7. G	8. 葡萄酒	9. 自転車	10. D	11. 夫	12. 人間
13. 愛人	14. F	15. 革命	16. 樺太犬	17. 盆栽	18. B
19. 決断	20. 抱擁	21. I	22. 余剰資金	23. H	24. 光
25. 泳ぐ	26. 手	27. 熱帯雨林	28. A	29. 投資	30. 接吻

Translated by Peter Robinson and Andrew Houwen

Noriko Ibaragi (1926–2006) is, together with Shuntarō Tanikawa, the
most highly regarded and popular poet of post-war Japan. She has
had an immense impact on contemporary Japanese poetry and her
collections have sold in the millions. Her two earliest collections
embody a new generation's desire to blossom out of the war's rubble
and celebrate the beauty of the human and natural universe. 'Fruits'
is from her second collection, *Invisible Messengers* (1957).

'Cherry' is from her seventh poetry collection, *The Drifting Smell of
Coffee from the Dinner Table* (1992). It was during this time that her
work established her towering reputation in the Japanese poetry
world. In the same year, Peter Robinson and Fumiko Horikawa
published the first collection of Ibaragi's work in English. We are
currently collaborating on a substantially enlarged and revised
selection from across her entire oeuvre.

Fruits

Apricot

In Amori village, Shinano, apricots grow.
Many come to paint, in my heart's gallery too.
Apricot flowers in a small picture frame
blossom, scatter, bear fruit.

Grape

Fresh-picked grapes tremble in my hands
like little birds, in whichever bag their purples show,

like that beautiful but fleeting time
of a young girl's heart and body.

Plum

I buy a great many plums in summer
to feel that I'm alive,
to remember the wartime defeat, the sorrow
when a plum was worth more than a ruby.

Chojuro Pear

With rope belt and snotty nose, the child
on a village road is holding you.
When biting into you, pale sweetness,
back come ancient, vanished Eastern tales.

Mandarin

When smelling mandarin flowers one year
I fell in love for the very first time.
I didn't know how to do it right then.
Even now they release that youthful fragrance.

Fruit with Forgotten Name

That fruit you would pawn your wife for,
fruit with forgotten name, fruit of a southern tree,
where was that tree, filled with seduction?
Whatever I do ends up in despair.

Cherry

Living this year
and seeing the blossom
one person in a lifetime
how many times do you see the cherry blossom
if grown aware of it first at, say, ten –
then around about seventy maximum,
some only thirty maybe forty,
what a small number!
The sense of it seen many, many more times
is a mingling, accumulating mist
of our ancestors' visions:
though eerie, weird, bewitching,
the gathering colour,
when tentatively treading under blizzards of petals
in a moment –
an illustrious monk – you realise
it's death is the ordinary condition,
and life a tender mirage.

Hearing Beyond the Darkness

Last year, I was asked to co-translate a poem by the contemporary poet Kei Okamoto. Opening the attachment, I found myself immediately drawn in: its weaving together of simplicity and mystery as it recorded the dissolution of (what passes for) a normal relationship between self, language and world made me think, amongst other things, of T.S. Eliot and Japanese concrete poetry. And yet I was aware, even as I dashed off a breathy 'yes please!' email, that this poem was not going to be easy to translate. The tortured nature of the speaker's connection with the world, which is evident from the beginning, intensifies throughout the poem, ultimately disintegrating entirely so the last few lines of the Japanese read as a scattering of single characters: constituent elements of words and phrases used previously, some words in their own right, others not, but now resembling seedlets drifting free of a dandelion clock.

This was my first experience of translating poetry with a strong visual element, and it left me with lots to mull over. In particular, the final section, where the poem breaks down into single glyphs: some in katakana, but most of them Chinese characters. As a literary translator, I'm used to feeling cowed by the possibilities of the Japanese toolkit, the tonal range offered by its three alphabets. A Japanese writer can, for example, cram a text with Chinese characters to make it more academic sounding, use words derived from English to make it trendy or pretentious, defamiliarise and poeticise words that are standardly written in Chinese characters, opt for katakana – the script used for foreign words, product names and so on – to create an emphatic or humorous effect, all functions which have no easy analogue in English. But now I was thinking about the characters in a more reductive way, which I rarely did when dealing with prose. Specifically, about how much more versatile they were as

building blocks than the ones with which English is built. A letter of
the alphabet is mostly just a letter, whereas every member of the
katakana or hiragana is already readable as a syllable, a sound. Then
there were the Chinese characters, or logographs, which had not only
associated sounds, but also meanings. How best to render an atomic
unit of this kind, one of Okamoto's single seedlets, in English?

This train of thought led me to concrete poetry, and how well-
suited Japanese is to it as a language. In particular, I recalled my first
encounter with the work of Seiichi Niikuni, the birth mother of
Japanese concrete poetry – the sense of delight that bubbled up when
I saw his poem 'Kawa mata wa su' (River/Sandbank). It takes the form
of a square split diagonally in half, the left-hand triangle made up of
tight rows of the character for river, which is itself composed of three
lines in a row: 川. The other diagonal half is made up of the character
for sandbank, similar to river but with dashes in between to represent
terrain: 州. (In fact, it can also mean 'country' or 'state', which has the
reading 'shū'.) The genius comes from the texture that it generates:
the density of the sandbank character in comparison to the river one
means that, when all these characters are lined up, they take on an
entirely different textural quality to the smoother, less hectic flowing
lines of the water. It is hard to envisage how one could ever hope to
'translate' this poem. It is writ large on the side of a building in
Leiden, the Netherlands, which features a 'key' in Dutch and English,
and indeed this seems like the only solution which could maintain
the textural impact of the original – although, of course, the experi-
ence of the viewer unused to dealing with these characters as
elements of their writing system is likely to be less rich than someone
who handles them on a daily basis.

Another favourite of mine from Niikuni's oeuvre focuses on the
character for darkness (闇; yami), composed of the radical for gate
(門; mon) with the character for sound (音; oto) sheltering inside it.

In Niikuni's poem *Yami*, we have a broad horizontal strip of the character for 'gate', with a large wall of 'sound' underneath it. Only a single middle row combines the two: a band of dense darkness, yami, that separates the gates from the sound.

I would like to go on, describing more of Niikuni's concrete poems; to speak of how they are simultaneously playful and profound. Concrete poetry plies language in the way a sculptor plies his material; I would like to talk about how the textural qualities of the script the concrete poet uses as their material impacts on their work. How here, the sheer impossibility of the task of translation feels somehow at its greatest, or at least raises its head in a new guise – and that this was the same sense present to me in diluted form in the Okamoto poem.

But as I do, I'm confronted by a sense of growing discomfort. Because here's the thing: the act of focusing on, fetishising, romanticising the visual elements of Japanese poetry is a practice that lies at the heart of the exoticising gaze. It is a way of thinking whose exaggerated expression we find in Ernest Fenollosa, whose work on Chinese poetry formed the basis for Ezra Pound's *Cathay*. 'You will ask,' Fenollosa addresses his reader, 'how could the Chinese have built up a great intellectual fabric from mere picture writing?' 'In what sense can verse, written in terms of visible hieroglyphics, be reckoned true Poetry?' To the questions he places in his reader's mouth, Fenollosa, as sinologist, provides answers. Lamenting the way Western culture has overlooked the potentiality of Japanese and Chinese poetry, he waxes lyrical about the rich imagistic resources that they have to offer, in a manner that now reads questionably. Further, in homing in on the grammatical, typographical elements of his subject, Fenollosa appears to forget that this poetry forms part of a language which has always been spoken, which has sound – that the characters he is dealing with, while not phonetic in the same sense as the Roman alphabet, are still, nonetheless, the written expression of a living, spoken culture.

Over a century has passed since Fenollosa's essay, and we in the translation field consider ourselves more aware of the dangers of the orientalising impulse and colonising gaze. Yet to my shame, it was only recently that a linguist friend reminded me, while I talked of this essay, that not only is the use of 'ideogram' and 'ideograph' as catch-all terms to describe Chinese characters incorrect, it is also indicative of this same orientalising gaze. For while Chinese characters do include pictograms (characters depicting the objects they describe) and ideograms (those representing their concepts), a majority of them are compounds of other elements, most often phono-semantic compounds which combine an ideographic element with a phonographic one. They are not, in other words, reducible to ideographic constituents; their visual formation is caught up with their pronunciation. Of course, linguistic terms are easy enough to muddle for those not well-versed in the terrain, but this particular mistake seems entrenched in a certain mentality: it buys in, once again, to the 'mere pictures' view of logographic languages.

Honestly, at that stage, I think about giving up on this essay, mostly out of fear. Fear of fetishising, which is the last thing I want to do; fear of being the person at the party talking about 'little pictures'. What saves me in the end is my books of poetry in translation, into which I retreat. It's the work of Sawako Nayakasu, her experiments with scripts in her translations and anti-translations of modernist poet Chika Sagawa. It's the translation of Yoshimasu Gozo's book, *Alice Iris Red Horse*, where a plethora of different creative techniques are called upon by a host of translators to recreate the wildly experimental visual and sonic aspects of Gozo's work. It's their common sense of wonder and committed experimentation around typographical, visual and many other aspects, in the hope of delivering to readers glimmers of associations that the original poems spark off. In fact, the thing that gives me most courage is an essay by poet and novelist Yoko Tawada which narrates her feeling upon encountering the German poet Paul Celan that he was 'peering into Japanese'. Tawada is fascinated by the Japanese translation of his volume *Von Schwelle zu Schwelle* (From Threshold to Threshold), and the way that a certain pictographic element pops up over and over: 'how is it possible that in this thin volume of poems, ideograms using the radical *gate* keep turning up at all the most crucial junctures?' The miraculous fact that, writing in German, Celan seemed to anticipate his translation into Japanese – to anticipate the 'decisive role' that would be played by the radical gate – Tawada finds in this serendipitous occurrence not only joy, but also understanding. A particular Celan poem, 'Von Dunkel Zu Dunkel' (From Darkness to Darkness), gives her the following insight into the composition of the character for darkness, yami – the same character to which Niikuni dedicated his poem:

> After reading this poem, I explain to myself the puzzling character 闇 as follows: That which can no longer be represented by *language*, the *darkness*, presumably lies behind the *gate*, but it isn't possible to peer through this *gate* because a sound is standing in the way [i.e. directly beneath the *gate*]. At the same time, there is a fear that it would be impossible to gain access to the darkness at all if this sound were no longer to exist. The sound is blocking the *gate*, but it is also the medium connecting this side of the *gate* with the other side. One must hear it, then it will no longer impede one's vision.

There could be no better introduction than Tawada's to the kinds of small miracles that translation can occasion: the new connections and understandings that you would never have thought possible before they happen. It seems to me, also, that Tawada's discovery about yami – 'one must hear it, then it will no longer impede one's vision' – also provides a perfect manifesto of how it is that we are to navigate the terrain of visual poetry. 'My poems are not to be read like traditional poetry,' stated Niikuni. 'You can read them from wherever you like, and think about them however you like.' Yet he was clear that he didn't want his poems to be thought of as art: they were not pictures, they were poems. His 1963 collection, *Zero-on* (Zero Sound), was split into two sections: the former containing visual poetry and the latter aural, but the former came accompanied by the instruction to read the poems aloud. Yes, the concrete poets may have treated words like matter, plying them with an awareness of their visual dimension, but they didn't do away with the sound.

In fact, I want to go further and say this: in concrete poetry, in any poetry with a visual element, the magic of the visual aspect exists in part because of language's phonic function. The reader or viewer of 'River/Sandbank' derives joy from seeing its elements pass from being meaningful words that can be enunciated, to being lines in a picture, and then back again, a bit like Wittgenstein's duck/rabbit. For most of us, reading is an activity inextricable from the act of hearing, of voicing – from the potentiality of being able to read something aloud. Yes, some concrete poetry – for example some of Niikuni's, which pulls the characters apart into elements that are no longer speakable – seems to drag the written words away from the spoken realm, but this is thrilling at least in part because of how they sit upon that cusp between being words and being other things, because the reader/viewer is watching this shift as it happens.

Now, thanks to Tawada, I think of the translator standing by the gate, in the darkness. The darkness is the impossibility of our task, the impossibility of representing one thing in a different way. And yet, as translators often declare, that site of impossibility is in fact a site of intense creative fertility. We need to work hard. To deal with difference, to fully absorb all of its potential for revolutionary suggestion without othering it takes constant work – the legwork of creativity, and also of listening. We work so that we can translate better. Which means: listen better, see better, play better.

References:

Yoko Tawada, 'Celan Reads Japanese', trans. Susan Bernofsky, in *The White Review*

Ernest Fenollosa, 'The Chinese Written Character as a Medium for Poetry' in *The Chinese Written Character as a Medium for Poetry*, with a foreword and notes by Ezra Pound, ed. Saussy, Stalling, and Klein, Fordham University Press, 2008.

Seiichi Niikuni, as quoted in the Seiichi Niikuni Edge Special, http://edgeofart.jp/コンクリート・ポエトリー新國誠一の楽しみ方/

The Niikuni poem refered to in the essay can be seen in situ in Leiden at: https://commons.wikimedia.org/wiki/File:Seiichi_Niikuni_-_Rivier-zandbank_-_Pieterskerkgracht_17,_Leiden.JPG

Translated by Motoyuki Shibata and Polly Barton
first published in *Hanatsubaki* (Shiseido Corporate Culture Magazine)

Our Whereabouts

don't speak to me   one whisper will change everything
why does   everyone   carry monsters around with them   so patiently
before my eyes   *the garden of vertigo* is *starting out at a blank sheet*
the moment   the words float up   I   brush against a soft breeze
catch alight   leaping flames   grasp at *the curtain of meadow*
grasp at *the flowerless bough*
words   grasp other words   one after another
but what is *the garden of vertigo?*
at each stand-still   the flint of the words   and the flint of the landscape   collide
snap crackle   tut-tut of tongues   here, you see?   I'm hearing things
I am   whispered to
leap up, little wisp of flame! stretch up, sweet chimney! the whole line blazes up
from the hem
starting out at a blank sheet blazes   *the flowerless bough* blazes
the deranged forest road blazes   *the dance of the imps* blazes
and though I am there   as though I was always meant to be   utterly lost
I can't find the words   ummmm   ummm
ummmm   ummmm
the garden of vertigo   taken out (burnt) from the oven   is

<pre>
                    whisp   ear
flint   er
            ear
                        ear
                                              er
hear   wisp

fire   tongue
        ear   ear
                                     er
</pre>

CHŪYA NAKAHARA

Translated by Jeffrey Angles

In even the smallest bookstores in Japan, one inevitably finds the work of Chūya Nakahara (1907–37), a passionate poet who has inspired generations of readers to fall in love with poetry. Even though Chūya was born over a century ago and died young at age thirty, he remains one of Japan's best-known modern poets – the subject of numerous biographies, studies, creative works, manga, and even a recent opera. Born in Yamaguchi in southwestern Japan, Chūya became fascinated at a young age with European modernism, especially Dadaism, and during the 1920s, he filled notebooks with experimental poems, which only came to light long after his death. In 1934, he published the subdued, melancholic collection *Yagi no uta* (Song of the Goat), which contains all of the poems translated here. As he lay ill from tuberculosis at the end of his life, his friends helped compile his second collection *Arishi hi no uta* (Songs of Days Gone By), but he died before it came out. Chūya was a great admirer of Arthur Rimbaud, whom he translated into Japanese and published in 1933. Because Chūya was so influenced by Rimbaud's voice and style, the translations included here of 'Overcast Sky' and 'Upon This Bit of Soiled Sadness' attempt to use meter and rhyme like Rimbaud. Indeed, the kind of dramatic, rhythmic regularity one finds in these poems is one reason these poems all have been set to music multiple times.

Overcast Sky

one morning   I saw   a black flag
fluttering   up there   in the sky
   the flag fluttered   back and forth   back and forth
inaudible   for it was   so high

   I wanted   to reel   it down
but without   any rope   how could I?
   so the flag   just fluttered   back and forth
dancing   into the depths   of the sky

   I recall   as a boy   many times
looking up   such mornings   back a while
   I saw one   that time   over the fields
now   once again   over city roof tiles

   this time   and that time   are so far apart
and this place   and that place   are not the same
   but oh black flag!   even now you flutter   all alone
back and forth   in the sky   unchanged!

Hangover

Morning, a dull sun shines
The wind blows
A thousand angels
Play basketball
I close my eyes tight
Such a sad hangover
The stove I no longer use
Grows white with rust
Morning, a dull sun shines
The wind blows
A thousand angels
Play basketball

Upon This Bit of Soiled Sadness...

Upon this bit of soiled sadness
The flurries fall again today
Through this bit of soiled sadness
The wind blows again today

This bit of soiled sadness
Not unlike a foxling's fur
This bit of soiled sadness
Catches snow, huddles and curls

This bit of soiled sadness
Has neither wishes nor desire
This bit of soiled sadness
Dreams of death in languor

This bit of soiled sadness
Tragic, strikes me with fright
This bit of soiled sadness
Helpless, enveloped by night...

ITSUKO ISHIKAWA

Translated by Rina Kikuchi and Jen Crawford

Itsuko Ishikawa's 'For You' reflects on the Kantō Massacre of 1923, in which more than 6,000 Korean residents of Japan were murdered. In the days following the Great Kantō Earthquake, fires proliferated, water and food supplies were cut off, and many newspapers stopped printing. Amid the chaos, rumours were circulated that Korean residents were rioting and planning terrorist attacks by arson and the poisoning of wells. Police, army and vigilante groups carried out lynchings and mass executions of those they identified as Korean. In its aftermath, the massacre was concealed by the Japanese government, with the nature of the events and the numbers of dead unclear.

Further reading:

Ryang, Sonia. 'The Great Kanto Earthquake and the Massacre of Koreans in 1923: Notes on Japan's Modern National Sovereignty.' *Anthropological Quarterly* Vol. 76, No. 4 (Autumn, 2003).

Kato, Naoki. *Trick: Those who Deny The Korean Massacre*. Tokyo: Koraka, 2019.

For You

—*who were massacred on the riverbanks of Nakagawa and Arakawa, after the Great Tokyo Earthquake, 1 September, 1923.*

What am I meant to do?
You were buried ten years before I was born.

The riverbed's full
of your formless faces.

Your compatriots who search for you
call this place *Teki-kyo*, enemy-capital.

I call out for you
without your names,

you, with your arms tied behind you,
you, butchered by hatchets,

you, shot
and kicked to the river,

you, pregnant
and young,

you, who came to study,
you were there too,

and you, yoked to a cart because
your cropshare was taken by a Japanese loanshark.

Tens of thousands of years ago
pictures were drawn of the great fallow deer.
They can still be seen with infra-red

but I can't know you, who died sixty years ago,
how many you are – hundreds? more? – or your names.

What am I meant to do?
You're buried in wretched longing

while we serenely cross the Nakagawa
and stroll through the town of Kameido.

What are we meant to do?
September's here again, the canna lily blooms

while you of the neighbouring land, your names and wrath
bleed into the riverbed.

For more than half a century
we have trampled over you.

Translated by Eric E. Hyett & Spencer Thurlow

Toshiko Hirata is a Japanese poet, playwright, and author, and is well
known as a member of the 'women's boom' of Japanese poetry
beginning in the 1980's, along with Hiromi Ito and others. These
poems come from her award-winning 2004 collection *Is It Poetry?*

On her source of inspiration for this work, Hirata explains that
once, while struggling with motivation, she asked her editor if she
should really keep writing at all, or just return to her hometown and
find another job. Her editor replied that she could keep writing if she
wanted to or not, but ultimately the world would not be affected by
her decision either way. Frustrated by this indifference, Ms. Hirata set
herself the task of writing a poem on the seventh day of the month,
every month, for two years. Her book therefore consists of 24 poems.

She committed hard to the task, expanding the traditional
concept of poetry by conjuring dramatic narrative situations that
border on the supernatural. In addition to deeply reflective personal
poems, she spends a fair amount of time borrowing from her own
words as a playwright and novelist. The Japanese title, *Shinanoka,* is a
pun: shinanoka means both 'poems on the seventh day' and 'is it
poetry?'

Is it January?

I'm going on a trip.
Just to write poetry.
That was my plan. But right away: setback.
Early evening-ish
I steal a seat on the subway;
My eyes fix
on *Elle Japon Monthly*'s
conspicuous pink
dangling ads
that say nothing to me.
Have I turned into a man?

I'm going on this trip.
Even if I have to be a man. Become a man,
literally just to write poetry.
Then, a thin voice:
I bought a Bear Hug Body Pillow because I was lonely.
So that's it! When a woman feels lonely, she buys a 'body pillow.'
I bet she cuddles that body to sleep.
Body = the torso apart from the head, neck,
arms, and legs : a sculpture of the trunk of the body. (Kojien
Dictionary)
I bet she enjoys buying stuff like that.
This subway line transports
men and women equally.
Though the place they feel vibration
is subtly different
for each person:

Men's stop
Women's stop
Men's stop
Women's stop
Trains stop in order
Men's stop
Women's stop
Men's stop
Women's stop
Reddish light tinges the Marunouchi Line
Men's stop
Women's stop
Men's stop
Women's stop
Before you know it, every passenger's
a Bear Hug Body Pillow.

Is It January Again?

I buy makeup
for someone in her seventies.
Liquid foundation
to cover up wrinkles and spots.

We first met when
this person was in her twenties,
unhappily married,
sullen-faced
changing her baby's diapers.

She wasn't any happier
in her thirties.
Her sewing machine
clacking out inconceivable things.

In her forties, she
secretly read her daughter's diary,
opened her daughter's letters without asking,
set a curse that her daughter should never be happy.
The curse worked extremely well.
The daughter suffered headaches every day.

I didn't know this person in her fifties.
I had moved far away.

I didn't know this person in her sixties.
I never went back even once.

By the time I met this person
twenty-something years later, she
was well into her seventies.
More old person than mother.
I was shaken.
I'd never expected the day
when my mother would be old.

Now, in my forties,
I read her shopping lists,
open her bills without permission
and pay them.
Though I haven't forgiven her
for what happened in her forties,
I still buy makeup for her
in her seventies.

Am I using this
liquid foundation
to cover up wrinkles and spots,
or to hide
my own feelings?

Translated by Mary Jo Bang and Yuki Tanaka

Shuzo Takiguchi (1903–1979) was one of the most prominent
Surrealists in Japan. He corresponded with the French Surrealists and
translated André Breton's 1928 *Surrealism and Painting* into Japanese
two years after it was published in France. In his own poems,
Takiguchi expanded on the surrealist mode of using dream-like
associative imagery by adding literary and philosophical allusions,
French and English words, invented personas, and comical puns. His
elaborate wordplay becomes an argument about how language works,
how poetry works, and especially about how the imagination works.
Embodied in that argument is a larger, political argument about the
freedom to be oneself.

Between 1937 and 1941, Takiguchi stopped writing poems and
devoted himself to corresponding with the French Surrealists,
translating their work, writing and publishing art criticism, and
curating exhibitions of Surrealist art. On March 5, 1941, Takiguchi
was arrested by a branch of the Police called *Tokko* – frequently
translated as 'Thought Police'– and held as a 'thought criminal,' a
category that included anyone influenced by the West. After his
release, on November 11, 1941, he wrote very few poems but instead
became a well-respected visual artist and art critic. In 1967, admirers
of his work collected the individual poems that had previously
appeared in magazines and published them as a book titled *The Poetic
Experiments 1927–1937.* 'The Royal Family of Dreams: A Manifesto, or
Regarding *A-priori* Dreams,' is included in that book. The poem was
as originally published in Japan in January 1930.

The Royal Family of Dreams: A Manifesto or Regarding A-priori Dreams

'...[J]ust as the Phoenix carries the secrets of its ashes inside it,' all discoveries are pregnant with the mystical force of the *siphonophore*, a bluebottle zooid-colony that lights up a whole illusionary May-Wine woods. Meanwhile, humans get tipsy on heaven-sent talent. The absolute senses, fascinated by objectivity, rip reality apart using the sky's own claws. O blueprint of a spider-web inked on the sky-blue sky and on its thriving cities. Where do the dazzling senses reside? Which heavenly body acts as a transparent gas-giant that pokes at the sky's open eye. The divinity of the acquired magical power is a free spirit that avoids every organized religion. O airborne god of tall tales flying there, O rose of lying, O outlandish hour, O conundrum!

There are calves that drink up every ray of light. There are pups that get drunk on every fine Bouzy champagne of the senses. Here the palm line gets so ecstatically looped it continues to hand-stitch whitecaps in a dream. There a mammalian moon smiles up. A volcanic vase was once an emperor's crown. O humanity that has a timeless memory regarding phenomenon, thou art shocked by thy humans. Startled by thy machines. Taken aback by thy capacity to invent. Thou art dazed by thy dreams. Now I invite a dream. A dream that emits light and roars inside an amorphous form. The offspring of a dream. The atmospheric phenomenon of a dream. The dream is an ability that is handed out. A scenic goldmine. If humans confuse the science of dreams and the dream of science, the history of art will have begun to be eclipsed. Eject the idea of dream from your concept. The dream will be resurrected.

The dream is the opposite of the absence of a dream, and action is the opposite of inaction. Obviously, dreaming and acting are incompatible. Like wormy vermicelli and caramel candy inside a seashell.

Treatise on Style, Louis Aragon

The dream was always the living room of inspiration. When lavish hair in a dream hangs down, you don't doubt your eyes. What rationale is there for these rhetorical terms? It comes closer to a type of dreamy reasoning. Upon waking one always suspects this *a-priori* ghost. Rather one embraces it. The logic of the senses is guided by the metaphysics of love. Against a backdrop of butterflies in flight. Who gave the consummate painter, painting in a dream as if inside a bottle of very fine wine, his skills. The dream's gift of know-how is a promise of Eros. A lovely circularity begins here. A dream only dreams up a surreal reality. A dream can be exchanged with nothing. It sits idly by. A thing without existence. Criticise dreams and you'll be cursed. You're an uncivilized churl who doesn't understand this unassailable science. For humans who are insensitive to these many marvels, versification, *Inferno*, *Paradiso*, and the phenomena of this very real material universe, it's hopeless for you to participate in the construction of a future world. And the human analysis of the illusionary pyramid teeters on the brink of destruction.

The image is an unparalleled means of expression promised to humans. Like love, the mind's demon that got bisected into two universes haunts the dots on dice and the revolving door's X. Right here a burning key was being grasped. And here too, the secret of an imposing haunted mansion was held onto. Just so, the inspiration for the image was the body. O phantom that gave its legs to Truth, my deformity is refined, thou art no longer of this realm, thy eyes can be mistaken for the Milky Way, thy hand is of the hardest tungsten, thou art not truly living, thou art only making an appearance, thou art dumbstruck. Thou art uncanny. The awareness of thee is inside my body. Only if thy five senses are my five senses, will I believe thou art appearing. Please pluck the stars inside me, stardust drifting down onto the brain-waves of my dreams.

Chirico did admit at that time he could only paint when *surprised* (first off surprised) by a confident positioning of things and that for him the whole of any disclosure of the enigma was contained in that word: surprised. To be sure, the resulting body of work remained 'intimately linked to what had provoked its being and birth,' but only resembled it 'in the queer way two brothers look alike,' or better yet, the dream image of a particular person and the real person. 'It is, at the same time it is not, one in the same person; a subtle and mysterious transfiguration is detected in the facial features.' On another level, underlying the arrangement of these things, which clearly for him displayed a flagrant peculiarity, it would still be necessary to fix critical attention on these objects themselves and to look into why these, so very few in number, have been called upon once again to lay themselves out like this. One will have said nothing about Chirico until one has taken into account his most subjective views on the artichoke, the glove, the biscuit or the bobbin.

Nadja, Andre Breton

There is the material world or the world of imagination. Imagination is a pan-spiritual phenomenon. This is the world of elements. The particular element, is that the mystery of the endless dream in a mirrored labyrinth? The spirit of the chase captivated by eternity always dives into the looking glass of the imagination. O funhouse mirror-room that baffled me there for a second, that was an irreducible see-through crystal. A dream in the end is indescribable. O inductive genius, his business is being the rubber glove and Roman artifact painter. The metaphysics of infancy presented him with one vast landscape of love. I will once again close the door of the labyrinth by quoting someone:

> For my part, I will continue to live in my glass house, where one can see at all hours who comes to visit me, where whatever is suspended from the ceiling and the walls is held there as if by magic, where I lie at night on a glass bed with glass sheets, where *who I am* will appear to me sooner or later engraved with a diamond.
>
> Nadja, Andre Breton

Here is a treasure chest of dreams. One's second nature is the first discovery. Listen to the dream gradually making its way to the shore. To him praising the colours of the whitecaps however he wishes, to him collecting seashells with his peculiar hands, to him impulsively whispering to the fish. For the first time, it's time for the dream to redistribute his blood. It's time his song is heard. Do-Re-Mi-Fa-Sol-La-Ti-Do. A blue dream concocts a collar for *Elle*. O the lovely sleeper's train of thought, O composition of a novel mist, the consequence of the dream was proof of pure phenomena. The dream, the idealized form of the truth, is eventually elbowed over to become the dream, the perceptible form of the truth. The moral of a dream tells one's inheritance. The recollected future is 'it's time' for a sleeper. Dreams incinerate instantly. At that moment, only the echo of matter stays forever to dance about without its shadow. Thus, the immortality of matter and the lyricism of physics was established.

The window moults. My might shakes me
Makes me stumble.

Love, Poetry Paul Éluard

Right here, a 'Snowball Rebellion' fairy seduces 'the persona-unknown
adventure butterfly | inside absurdist prisons.' That snowfall in the
Time-Space continuum was more than merely amazing. O humans
with your ancient sensory bodies, O humans with your ancient
survival instinct, the recycling of thy likeness is the human history of
starvation. The night of eternal love will continue without blinking to
keep its best *femme fatale* fireflies. Image is language:

> Éluard's poems [...] are like a keeper's jewelled watch-case for our
> secret, here yet again is a reason to live, which is just to say it is both
> a reason to keep having patience and to lose patience.
>
> *The Lost Steps,* André Breton

His 'deaf images' meet up with me when I dream. It was a transparent
coincidence. But when he was broken on the rock of his body, I didn't
yet exist. His dream has gone through more centuries than mine.
When I was still a mother-of-pearl particle, he must have been staring
at the sea like her Ladyship. While I was infantile, he must have been
contemplating.

He's the demon of the image. He's at the height of his nights and
rules. That is the world of imagination. Image is the beginning of
everything. This one is the one who's deaf. This one is the one who's a
demon. A real demon, now you doubt your own eyes. You'll escape into
your own objectivity. You, with no knowledge of what's behind the
mind of the maker.

Birds wider than winds
No longer know where to land.

Paul Éluard, from the periodical Variétés

◆

There was once a white prince in a black kingdom. He may only be able to exist in a fairy tale. Beyond an iceberg, it always has to be *beyond* wherever. The fire that melts that ice will never exist. O impoverished human intellect! With, however, the exception of the modern invention of one mental concept (i.e, *Beyond the Pleasure Principle*). Skeptics of that concept will be struck dead by lightning. That holy truth is [*Mama, Papa is Wounded*]. Mr. Yves Tanguy's children's fairy tale about unadulterated matter. The ruination of every perception has occurred. The panic-stricken state of every perception has occurred. His feelings don't yet have any redress on earth. Is his world harmonious? Rather, a ghost appeared out of reality. There was that business of a white shadow that looked a bit like a spider. I still don't see what type of love has been made under the stars of this fair hair. I only make out an elegant gravid physiology that seemed like an egg-shaped ritual. I see. I see. How different is this, for example, from just running with it? The white prince, he'll be listening to distant thunder. The far-off thunder will be transformed to white sap by his snow-white hand. Right here, for the first time, people perceived how malicious it is to doubt the senses. People heard for the first time a natural voice inside his agate cloud. People will now be unconsciously singed by other novel flashes of light. At that hour, he will plant a forest of trees in the sky. O miracle, dream lyricism! All language is an empty vessel. Egg-shaped dream, I adore the elliptical dream that spreads out toward a new world. O transcendental peace, complete thy egg-laying business. When I make a pout with my lips, look, a painting of a white-prince in a black kingdom lights up the colours of a rainbow.

◆

It is not in the nature of this coming Monday to insist the balcony absorb all the free CO_2 coming from a dolphin's blowhole. Part of the blizzard inside my humeral head is cutwork embroidery for this season's Eden. The volatility of a polar bear is the same as the surface of a lake in the north south east or west. Unending swarms of fireflies fly by & the great hero of the fluoroscopic image goes on living on a muddy-creek-beach. It's the aim of shelly-moonlight to shake ad infinitum the cactus of bright ideas. This is a silent strategy on a strand of gorgeous sand. The *pascal* of a penned-in diver, the same Pascal '[Man is . . . but] a thinking reed.' A fish is a lightning rod that understands the literal fits each letter to a T. The Cigar Galaxy chews over the fact earth is also an orb. The malicious idea that a heavenly body's emotions can only be shown when kept under its hat doesn't match up with the gentle bolt from the blue where the entire universe was out hunting. Sing this. You who came to look into the fiction of a chick singing her lungs out, spin your orb-like cheeks until they turn off-white. The pulsing of a pearl gives birth to a self. With a pacific feeling. Moreover, the ocean is current. Boas are au-courant. Triangles are new-fangled. Navels are cutting-edge. The mirror of the bellybutton is the only god of sensation. A rosy cactus with good skin in a lonely brave new world. Here is another cactus. The straight pins of the cactus become misted moons. It's rain. It's a state. A traveller-for-the-sake-of-travel casts his anchor in the shade of a wave. A British-blue cat in an absurdist dream, a new looking-glass in a *Narcissus*, the gravel's kid gloves, the raging billows of a triangle, are the secrets of the mice that rescued the dying *Elle* lying on a lonely shore. An anonymous mouse flies about in a colourless outhouse. A chaotic botanic garden is laid out in the Greek style. My hello is in the style of *Paradise* ['Say, Heavenly Powers, where shall we find such love?]. . . I proceed' to Eros.

◆

The crystal's already see-through by the time a breeze is blowing, long before mounting a white horse, I mounted a transparent horse. I inhaled crystal air, then blew it out. My rapid panting was the effect of the crystal. In a single night, I saw through to the end the principle of my vision with a fair-haired mouse. Neither Time nor Space can ever close off the beautiful adventure of that night's spirit. For the first time, the human will is connected to the future. This is not a theory of art. I'm one of those who saw a pearl necklace sway in a windless shop window. When every idea of art and every notion of life are dried up, an adventure-trip to the phenomenal world gets attempted. O astonishing view! O persistence of amber born in an unknown forest on a border, dost thou subsist on electric sparks? That young brain is brimming with blueprints for amazing cities. Fledgling birds and beasts run about. Near CO_2 columns, a fish with rose-coloured glasses writes a line of verse on a future-perfect riverbed. O here too is a dreaming firefly. O iodine boy. An eight-eyed lamprey-eel fantasizes facing a pure-yellow sky. That sense of nostalgia seems to be as ingrained as fool's gold. I along with other people never doubt this. On the horizon that again turns lucid red, countless lucid red goddesses beckon. The goddess that knows how to force wild cherry blossoms came over and led me to a desk under a sun-lamp. That, too, seems to have been only a rubric-red illusion. Crimson sex, blushing me. My scarlet magic gets born one beautiful night with an imagined spirit. Hey you, do you know the red fairy?

Suddenly, a captivating sediment demands my attention. Civilisation always hands out pleasure and displeasure at the same time. O magnesium level in your brain, O lamp in a pantheon. Make-up for the sake of make-up, that's architecture. Go public with your sensory awareness of heaven and your sensory awareness of hell. Religious retribution flows backwards.

All reason leads back to your creative optimism. God wriggles within you. The hope of a dream depends on the future of the over-and-above-history, and each dream is a newborn dream. At this point, I deny all absurdist conjectures about dreams. The time has come when the inspiration of a parti-coloured wagtail moves the gods. On the eve of an endless revolution, the ink of my mind is drenched with dream colours. The headwind of an unassailable dream flutters my lashes. O animals of objectivity high in the sky, O snail-grey monotony, try as you might to measure me. Try as you might to love me.

Translated by James Garza

Takuji Ōte (1887–1934) was born to an inn-keeping family in rural
Gunma Prefecture. While he published in some of the leading
journals of the day, his reputation as a pioneer of Japanese symbolism
is largely posthumous. As prolific as he was (with an output totaling
some 2,400 poems), he published no collections during his lifetime.
'Porcelain Crow' comes from his first posthumous collection, *Aiiro-no
Hiki* (Indigo Toad), which was compiled by his close friend, the artist
Henmi Takashi, in 1936. Ōte's symbolist poetics, informed by the likes
of Baudelaire and Samain, have attracted both Jungian interpreta-
tions and charges of obscurantism. From the standpoint of
representation, 'Porcelain Crow' is indeed obscure. But as Utsumi
Noriko has argued, this may be precisely where the greatest value
of Ōte's work lies: in emphasising the signifier over the signified, he
reaffirmed the importance of the materiality of words in creating
affect and mood.

Porcelain Crow

Blue porcelain crow,
on the make with your oohs and ohs –
Reeling with hatchling warmth.
Your big bill and eyes: a grifter's smile.
Go ahead, eat the silence of this hush.

SHUNTARO TANIKAWA

Translated by William I. Elliott and Katsumasa Nishihara

It is no accident that a series of poems that Shuntaro Tanikawa has been building, one a week, for several years now in the *Asahi Evening Newspaper,* is called 'Words from Somewhere', because that very title could well be the underlying clue to an understanding of his entire career as a poet. Since his first book appeared, in 1952, through to his latest, in 2019, he has been searching for words; or words have been successful in searching for him. Yet it is an astonishment that he has never been satisfied with words – his or anyone else's, for he views words as an impediment, as a wall that stands between the human being, who longs for direct hands-on experience, and the perceived exterior world. Communication, on account of words, is not barrier-free. Words, he says, fail at the same time that as a poet he is helplessly in their thrall. This now wistful, now frustrated assumption underlies all of his collections, that now number, by the way, more than sixty – sixty and counting.

A Single Line Is

A single line is standing
like a naked girl
on a snowy field of paper
without the poison of meaning.

An old *iroha*
is thrown away in the mountains.
A crowd of fonts
don't cry out loud.

Hidden in the solar plexus
of a premature baby
is a small, rainbow-coloured whirl
of words.

Ahead of
a single line standing motionless
are the rustle of leaves
and the sound of waves in the distance.

An Idea About an Angel (3)

An angel turns an innocent gaze
upon both the rich and the poor
without discrimination.
That's all it can do.
But a welfare office and a tax office collude in pretending
somehow that there exist no angels in the world.
But an angel does actually exist and is said to do something
when someone dies.
What it does will be known to you
just when you actually die.
'An angel is my drone,'
a boy jots down in his notebook,
'and I'll have it descend into Hell
by using a remote control device in my mind.'
A girl who happens to steal a glance at the notebook
silently shows him her selfie.
He cannot see on her shoulders
the wings which begin to grow.

A balsa plane powered by a rubber band
awkwardly circles around over the park
and plops into a pond.

Leave Me Alone Like This

Who's going to say
it's ok
to let me go on doing like this
in a voice like a tree's
and a whisper like rain's?

Parting with words
I listen to the sounds
at hand
while letting sorrow
be sorrow.

The right forefinger
used to point at someone
whose fingerprint reveals
the one and only
myself...

Under
the cloudy sky
I feel shame
at the beauty
of lies in poetry.

Innovation and Testimony

I Am a Rohingya: Poetry from the Camps and Beyond, edited by
James Byrne and Shezhar Doja with a preface by John Kinsella,
Arc Publications, 2019.

The first English-language anthology of Rohingya poetry, *I Am a Rohingya*,
is a necessary collection that displays the artistry of current Rohingya
poets alongside transcriptions of older orally-transmitted folk-songs
('riversongs'). The resulting body of work is a testimony to the variety of
Rohingya poetics, past and present, while also a chronicle of the Rohingya
people's struggle in the face of genocide. The thirty-three poems that
comprise this collection are diverse in voice and form, rich in artistry,
and an important cultural record of a people that have been brutalized
and displaced. In his introductory essay, editor Shehzar Doja writes that
'The simple truth is that the ethnic Rohingya population, which has
existed for several centuries, was being systematically purged of its identity
including, essentially, its culture, in a manner reminiscent of great ethnic
purges of the past'. In this way, poetry becomes both an act of witness
and assertion of identity, a two-pronged approach that pushes against
cultural erasure and testifies to the Rohingya poets' experiences.

The editorial interventions, which include two essays and a full-length
interview between poet and activist Mayyu Ali and editor James Byrne,
provide succinct, in-depth background about the Rohingya people and
the ongoing crisis that they have faced. In brief, the Rohingya people are
a primarily-Muslim minority originating from the Rakhine State (Arakan)
in Myanmar. They have long faced discrimination by Myanmar's
government, being systematically denied freedom of movement, access
to higher education, and healthcare. Under a 1982 citizenship bill, the
Myanmar government declared that Rohingya people cannot hold
Myanmar citizenship; thus, they are not protected against discrimination

by the laws that apply to citizens – a form of legalised persecution. All of this background is necessary context to an informed reading of *I Am A Rohingya*. Mayyu Ali states that 'Writing for Rohingya people is activism', an ethos that is apparent throughout the collection. Most of the poets are refugees who have had to flee their homes in Arakan (the name that many Rohingya prefer over the Myanmar government's official name of the 'Rakhine State'). Indeed, many of the poems are first-hand accounts of the violence that the poets and people around them have experienced.

Several poems focus on grim descriptions of dehumanisation, ranging from the cruelty of discrimination (Thida Shania's 'First Day at School' and Pacifist Farooq's 'My Life') to the horrors of bloodshed (Yar Tin's 'About Those Born into This Place' and Mayyu Ali's 'They're Kind Killers'). Mayyu Ali's 'That's Me, A Rohingya' and Ro B. M. Hairu's 'Behind Life' relate first-hand encounters with injustice in stanzas that strategically repeat their structure and word choice. This technique is highly effective in building the poems' sensory impact. For example, in 'That's Me, A Rohingya', the organs of the body express the poet's reflections through neural responses:

> My skin trembles
> Just to feel once the full meaning of freedom,
> My heart wishes
> Just to walk once in my own world.

The use of anaphora evokes both crisis and exhaustion; in this way, the poetic form parallels the continued onslaught of trauma. Poems like Zaki Ovais's 'Water' and Ro B. M. Hairu's 'Tell Me What We Are Guilty Of!' build upon themselves, each line an echo that amplifies force of the poet's words. In 'Being Rohingya', Ro Anamul Hasan writes 'I was born in hell. | I was born in the bloodstream. | I was born on the battleground.' This list-like style is simple, yet chilling, as discrimination is described as a matter of routine.

Repetition as a literary device is also apparent in some of the poem titles, where the word 'Rohingya' arises again and again, sometimes as a prefix to the poets' names ('Ro') and, of course, in the title of the anthology itself. This assertion of cultural identity functions as self-assertion and preservation. It should be noted that the Myanmar government denies that Rohingya identity even exists, inaccurately (and strategically) referring to Rohingya people as Bengali. Within this context, the word Rohingya itself becomes a corrective against acts of erasure.

While the aforementioned poets employ repetition and linear forms for artistic effect, others conduct dynamic formal experiments. Weaving movement and fracture into their verses, pauses and breaks to force the reader's eye across the negative space of the page – an astute way of incorporating two primary motifs into the very structure of the poems themselves. In this way, poems like Maung Hla Shwe's 'An Orphan', Azad Mohammed's 'Misfortune', and Yasmin Ullah's 'The Unfamiliar Home' explore the spatial confines of the written page. Using sprawling stanzas that test the boundaries of the medium, these poems force the reader to move with the poet; the eye cannot remain stationary while reading, mirroring the familial and geographical displacement described. An example is Ullah's use of line breaks as she reflects upon the concept of 'home' in relation to diaspora:

I keep missing a place I barely know.

Home – untouched
families I can never return to,
how I long
        for their
                hugs.

Ullah's enjambments are wistful, evocative expressions of longing. The familial embrace is stretched across the page, far from reach, except in the poet's own mind. Other poets like Maung Abdul Khan take the opposite approach in 'New Hope' and 'Survivor'. Rather than being spread across the page, the poems are compact structures that resemble a sort of fortification. While both poems use short, terse syllables to create a sense of dislocation, 'New Hope' in particular uses dashes and line breaks to create an unstable rhythm that mirrors the poem's subject of interrupted motion:

> This journey – *anguished*
> I am – at the last – *stage*
> Facing | *failure*

The jarring stops and starts resemble shortness of breath. As the verses gasp between pauses, one must also share the poet's own movement and breath in order to engage with the poem. There is no passive perusal; the poem demands the reader's full engagement, and reading becomes an embodied function.

The final poem of the collection is Ro Mehrooz's 'Night-blooming Jasmine (Hasna Hena)', a work of melancholy beauty that reflects the poet's strong sense of place as he invites the moon to his sister's wedding:

> O moon uncle, moon uncle, please hear me.
> Come to the wedding wearing white.
> For you, the buds of the night-blooming jasmine wait.
> The wind will blow, blow slowly, the buds will fall.
> The whole fence will smell of its scent.

The lyrical construction and narrator's address to the natural world recall the three translated Rohingya riversongs present in this collection:

'Lovesong', 'Lament (A Fisherman's Song)', and 'Mother Arakan'.
Doja describes the riversongs as possessing 'a shared and sincere arc
of yearning and reflection'. Like 'Night-blooming Jasmine', the
riversongs imbue seemingly mundane subjects with a dream-like
quality. This is demonstrated in esoteric lines like '*I discover Hajera's
fragrance on the bird's handkerchief*' in 'Lovesong', and moments of
sinister strangeness in 'Lament':

> In just an empty boat
> A fisherman has stolen my soul

> That fisherman, he lures me   – *laughing, laughing*
> He draws me in with his eyes

'Night-blooming Jasmine' seems a contemporary riversong – a
modern continuation of a poetic tradition. Palpable with longing, the
poet's plea to the moon takes on a special significance alongside the
preceding accounts of displacement and bloodshed. Here, the poet
turns away from other people for a moment of solitary contempla-
tion, and calls instead to a celestial body for witness of a joyful event.
It is a haunting moment, but embedded with hope for future
happiness. In this way, the anthology ends with the promise of
continued innovation within a rich and resonant poetic tradition.

Sarah-Jean Zubair

Necessary Communication

Poetry of the Holocaust: An Anthology, edited by Jean Boase-Beier and Marian de Vooght, Arc, 2019.

Writing this review on the 75th anniversary of the liberation of Auschwitz, it feels important to consider ethics, as well as aesthetics. Commemoration ceremonies are broadcasting the testimony of the last few survivors, some of whom have chosen to finally make themselves heard as a warning to future generations, after many years of silence. Theirs was not the silence of inarticulacy or of fear but, as Howard Jacobson wrote in *The Guardian*, 'the silence of tact', a reticence he describes as 'a moral and psychological obligation'. He goes on to suggest that Adorno's famous phrase, 'no poetry after Auschwitz', can be read as an injunction or a lament. 'Either way, it didn't simply mean no fancy language. It meant not rushing to possess by articulation, or even to explain what might have been beyond explanation, while the thing itself was still warm and its consequences still unfolding.'

In their introduction to *Poetry of the Holocaust*, the editors Jean Boase-Beier and Marian de Vooght are less hesitant, indeed less reticent, than Jacobson (or Hilda Schiff, editor of the seminal anthology of Holocaust Poetry they mention as their inspiration) when it comes to post-Holocaust writing, claiming that 'Of course, Adorno was right to reject the aestheticizing of the Holocaust. But poems (and other forms of art) as necessary communication do not aestheticise.' Their statement can be read two ways. Either 1) poetry as a form is necessary communication and all poems, by virtue of being so, do not aestheticise or 2) that those poems which are, because of their poetic and historical integrity, necessary communication do not aestheticise and so are permissable. If the editors' intention is the latter, I agree with them, but on reading their anthology, it seems that their formulation may be the former, as they stretch the bounds of what has previously been considered Holocaust poetry away from the urgency of testimony.

I applaud their inclusion of a wider range of voices, particularly those who provide additional historical narratives that until now have been rarely heard in English. The editors have translated Sinti poet Philomena Franz and Roma poet Ceija Stojka, both of whom survived Auschwitz as well as other camps, and who lost immediate family members. In direct, simple language, they describe the extinguishing of their childhoods: for Franz, 'hope [...] forced me to live' but today 'I see the light of too many scars', a response opposite to that of Stojka whose 'fear stayed behind in Auschwitz | and in the camps'. Read alongside the raging anger of József Choli Daróczi's 'In memory of the gypsy victims of the Holocaust', powerfully translated from the Hungarian by Jamie McKendrick, George Gömöri and Mari Gömöri, these poems urgently convey a sense of the harm done to that community.

There are other 'memorial' poems like Daróczi's, written by those who came later, notably André Sarcq's long poem, 'To the twice-murdered men (the Rag)'. It honours Pierre Seel, the first gay survivor to speak about his experience. Aged 18, Seel was sent to the concentration camp Schirmeck, where he was forced to watch as his lover, Jo, was killed by dogs. Two of Sarcq's epigraphs are taken from Celan, and the driven repetitions and vocabulary in lines such as 'Yes we are here | mass of outcasts from the memory of the just |alien snow beneath the snow of the Jews | black snow | black snow blackened by the ashes' clearly owe a debt to his 'Death Fugue'. While Celan's poem is partially about its own inarticulacy, Sarcq's is a hyper-articulate challenge as to why gay male history of the Holocaust has been so little spoken about.

But then there are inclusions such as Nitsa Dori, a Sephardi poet writing in Ladino who was also born after liberation, in 1960. She has two poems included, translated by Anna Crowe. Both are written in the first-person plural, claiming a universal voice. In 'Tell us no more train stories' she seems to speak for her own generation, addressing survivors with the plea to 'stop remembering the smoke at least | and don't talk about those in charge'. Instead 'let us weep for you | with tears of love.' In context of the Holocaust this seems to undermine the push for meticulous, truthful testimony. Instead, and I return to Jacobson, it 'angles for those double tears that are the hallmark of kitsch: weeping over the suffering of others and weeping a second time over our capacity to do so.'

In her other poem, 'If I did not believe in you...', where the 'you' is God, Dori's 'us' becomes the voice of the survivors themselves: 'in the camps you might have saved us | but you left us to be killed'. It finishes with her prayer 'let the little ones, the weak, | let them be saved'. Contrast this with Elie Wiesel's famous, wryly humorous, account of how he and his fellow Auschwitz inmates put God on trial and found him guilty on all charges, then went off to afternoon prayers, and Dori's words feel trite, appropriating a voice to which she has no right. Perhaps this is not the sense of the original, but in English, even if she were second generation with a family history of the Holocaust, this seems to cross the line. The editors don't give us information about whether Dori has immediate personal connections – an instance where more thorough notes would have been helpful.

In the 2008 anthology *Un grito en el silencio,* Shmuel Refael Vivante collected 100 Judeo-Spanish poems on the Holocaust, many worthy of a wider audience, so there is no lack of options in Ladino. I focus on Dori because I'm puzzled about why she was chosen, since her universalising perspective doesn't accord with the *ars poetica* set out in the introduction: 'Like all poetry, Holocaust poetry uses poetic means to create an impression, convey feeling, or to create such feeling in its readers. But it is responding to catastrophic and specific events.

Thus it tends not to generalise, but to particularise.' The editors illustrate this point with examples of eyewitness testimony by Bonhoeffer, Adler and Sutzkever. 'In these poems', they rightly say, 'the individual voice is everything'. All three of these poems, the first two from German and the third from Yiddish, are meticulously translated by Boise-Beier, especially Sutzkever's 'To the Child', a lyric elegy for his newborn son, murdered by the Nazis on the 18th January 1943: 'I wanted to engulf you, my child, | to feel how your tiny body grew cold | in my fingers, |as though I held fast in them | a warm glass of tea | and felt its transition to cold.'

Another poem about the relationship between father and son that is a welcome addition to the canon of Holocaust poetry is by Yukiko Sugihara, wife of a Japanese diplomat to Lithuania, Chiune Sugihara who, despite strict instructions from his government, issued transit visas to people fleeing the Nazis. The Japanese original is made of four tanka, that are translated into English as a single poem by Hadley and Regan. In careful, stepped lines, we're told how:

Fretting on visa decisions,
                  restless –
                              I hear my husband's bed creak.
In the flock of people awaiting visas,
                  an infant, his face dirty,
                        kneads his father's hand.

According to accounts elsewhere by Yukiko and others, Chinue initially intended to follow orders until his young son asked him why there were queues of people around the embassy. When his father explained, the son trustingly assumed that his father would save them, triggering three weeks of frantic stamping of papers that saved thousands. It is interesting that this translation seems to relocate the

infant son within the queue. I wonder if instead it should be some-
thing like 'Seeing the flock of people [....] an infant kneads his father's
hand', or are they perhaps faces in the crowd that remind Yukiko of
her own husband and son? Notes would have been helpful here for
readers who have no external frame of reference.

If Holocaust poetry is indeed a specific genre that necessitates
reading for historical content not just poetic skill, it is impossible to
perform a 'Death of the Author' style untethered reading. The brief
2–3 line introductory notes to each poet are unsatisfying and hint at
a lack of space. Yet this is a 241-page publication which crams in a
lot. I am grateful for its breadth of approach, and that it is a fully
multilingual edition, with each poem also reproduced in its original
language. However, I wish there were fewer poems, more carefully
contextualised and framed, each surrounded by the white space
such sensitive material needs to be properly digested. What we are
presented with is simultaneously a gift to future readers and a
collection that frustratingly obscures the very material the editors
are convinced, and have convinced me, it is absolutely necessary
to communicate to a wider audience.

Aviva Dautch

Elaine and Marina

In the 1971 Poetry International issue of
MPT, sponsored by Benson and Hedges
and bound in gold cigarette box card,
there is a glamorous picture of Elaine
Feinstein, advertising her most recent
novel (the same photo is on the cover of
her 2017 'New and Selected' *The Clinic,
Memory*). Her head is slightly bent to
take a drag on a newly-lit cigarette and
her thickly-lashed eyes are shut, as if
thanking the gods for this brief moment
of calm. The profile is elegant – the
heavy stone of the earring, the twist of

smoke and her closed eyes – but it's also full of restless energy: her
workmanlike fingers and tousled hair. It's this combination of
elegance and determined energy which, for me, characterised
Feinstein's writing life, and the way in which Feinstein set about
translating Marina Tsvetaeva is the perfect example of this.

In an *Essay in Autobiography*, published in English translation in
1959, the Russian poet Boris Pasternak wrote of Tsvetaeva that she
'soared over the real difficulties of creation, solving its problems
effortlessly and with matchless technical skill'. Pasternak had
intended this essay, with its descriptions of his spiritual and artistic
influences, to form the foreword to a late collection of poetry, but the
collection never materialised. Instead the prose was published in the
West in the wake of the publication of *Doctor Zhivago* and his forced
refusal of the Nobel Prize, and it was widely and eagerly read.

Feinstein was inspired by Pasternak's ecstatic description of this
unknown poet, and felt compelled to read her, 'perhaps to learn from

her'. When she discovered Tsvetaeva had not yet been translated into English, she got hold of a copy of the first, and only recently published, Soviet edition of her poems, and began working with the scholar and translator Angela Livingstone on translations, producing a body of work which was published in 1971 as *Marina Tsvetaeva: Selected Poems* by OUP. At least one of the long poems, 'The Poem of the End', was published in 1970 in *Modern Poetry in Translation*.

Feinstein did not speak Russian and so she worked with a number of Russianists, foremost amongst whom was Angela Livingstone. In the OUP edition Angela's notes on the process indicate the level of support Elaine received: meticulously annotated 'literals' indicated inversions, syntactic shapes and words like pronouns and articles which wouldn't have been present in the Russian.

The resulting translations are careful and researched, but they also have their own warmth and emotional intelligence and I'd like to use the opening stanzas of 'The Poem of the End' to briefly consider Feinstein's approach and the ways in which her translations assert themselves as independent entities.

In the English the opening lines have alternate rhyme on the second and fourth line and they read:

> A single post, a point of rusting
>   tin in the sky
> marks the fated place we
>   move to, he and I
>
> on time   as death is
>   prompt   strangely
> too smooth the gesture of
>   his hat to me

Feinstein uses spacing and indents to loosen the syntactic fabric of the poem, and lower case at the beginning of the lines; whereas Tsvetaeva's verse is capitalised and maintains a visual, as well as metrical, coherence and full alternate rhyme, ABAB. The Russian 'jolts and disturbs' in different ways: Tsvetaeva's use of traditional versification merely serves to point up the un-traditional ferocity, fragmentation and strangeness of the utterance confined within the structure, and Feinstein clearly had to find other ways to convey the oddness of tone and chafing frictions. She opted for a more modern appearance on the page, a shape that could be grasped, but was elegantly loose, something akin to the taut spaciness of Niedecker's long poems.

In the second stanza Feinstein takes the more radical decision to remove dialogue; dialogue being a structuring principle of this long poem, which describes a parting between two lovers. A more literal translation might read:

> 'Quarter to? All set?'
> 'Death doesn't wait.'
> Exaggeratedly low
> The ascent of his hat.

I instinctively feel that Feinstein's decision is based on the need to keep the reader held; that the phrasing feels too instantly and emphatically self-dramatising: *death doesn't wait* (Tsvetaeva never pulls her punches). There's also a consideration to be made: these are the first translations, they have to win an audience, this voice has to be heard and taken seriously, and Feinstein puts all her novelistic and poetic skills into making this compelling drama. As Livingstone generously writes in her Notes: 'All this *material* was then changed into poetry by Elaine Feinstein...'

Translating Tsvetaeva was not simply a duty or a day job for Feinstein. In an essay written for *MPT* in 1996 she notes that she recognised something in Tsvetaeva's work: 'an unguarded passion, and a desperation that arose from it, which was willing to expose the most undignified emotions'. In the late sixties, as Feinstein worked on the translations, there were few role models for a woman poet, a handful of 'devoutly Christian' and 'spinsterly figures', as she put it thirty years later, and Feinstein felt very much an outsider in a male world of contemporary poetry. In her translations of Marina she forges a new English-language voice and identity for women poets and for herself: a risk-taking, no-holds-barred identity; a modern voice whose internal dramas are projected large as shadow theatre on the page. The approach paid off. These translations were important, and not only to Feinstein herself – many other poets were liberated by Tsvetaeva's unbridled and extraordinary poetics in Feinstein's persuasive translation for the times. At an evening dedicated to Tsvetaeva, the poet Wendy Cope spoke of the revolutionary effect of Feinstein's translations and the way they gave her permission to have a woman's voice in poetry.

There have been other translations of Tsvetaeva, and there will be more. But in the months following Elaine Feinstein's death I have been reflecting on how her chance encounter with Tsvetaeva, and her subsequent serious commitment to translating her, made British poetry all the wilder.

Sasha Dugdale

NOTES ON CONTRIBUTORS

CLARISSA AYKROYD grew up in Victoria, Canada and now lives in London, where she works as a publisher. Her poetry has appeared in UK and international journals, and her pamphlet *Island of Towers* was published by Broken Sleep Books in 2019.
www.thestoneandthestar.blogspot.co.uk

HASAN ALIZADEH (b. 1947) has left a poetic signature on modern Persian poetry through his two volumes of poetry: *Rūznama-yi tab ʿīd* (Diary of House Arrest), 2003, and *Ducharkha-yi ābī* (Blue Bicycle), 2015.

JEFFREY ANGLES is an award-winning translator of Japanese literature and a professor at Western Michigan University. He writes poetry in both English and Japanese.

MARY JO BANG is the author of eight books of poems and a translation of Dante's *Inferno*, with illustrations by Henrik Drescher. She teaches at Washington University in St. Louis.

POLLY BARTON primarily translates Japanese fiction and non-fiction, and has featured in *The White Review, Granta*, and *Words Without Borders*. Recent publications include *Where the Wild Ladies Are* by Aoko Matsuda, from Tilted Axis Press.

CHRIS BECKETT is a poet and translator based in London. His last collection was *Ethiopia Boy*, published by Carcanet in 2013.

JEN CRAWFORD teaches writing at the University of Canberra. She is the author of eight poetry books and chapbooks, and co-edited *Poet to Poet: Contemporary Women Poets from Japan* (Recent Work Press, 2017) with Rina Kikuchi.

BEI DAO is one of China's most important authors. In the 1970s and '80s, he was a leading member of the avant-garde movement Ménglóng Shi Rén, or 'Misty Poets,' so-called for the abstract language and obscure meaning in their poems.

AVIVA DAUTCH is Lecturer in Modern Jewish Literature at the London School of Jewish Studies and Visiting Lecturer in Jewish Culture and the Holocaust at the University of Roehampton. Her poems are published in *Primers Volume Three* (Nine Arches Press: 2018).

SASHA DUGDALE is a poet and translator. Her translations of Maria Stepanova are published in 2020 by Fitzcarraldo Editions and Bloodaxe Books.

EFE DUYAN is a poet based in Istanbul, born in 1981. His poems have
been translated into nearly thirty different languages.

WILLIAM I. ELLIOTT and Kazuo Kawamura (d.2015) translated, starting
in 1968, some 50 of Tanikawa's collections. Elliott founded the Kanto
Poetry Centre and edited *Poetry Kanto* for twenty years.

KIT FAN is a Hong Kong-born poet and fiction writer. *As Slow As Possible*
is a PBS Recommendation and The Irish Times Best Poetry Book of
the Year. www.kitfan.net

BENJAMIN FONDANE (1898–1944), a Romanian Jew, began his literary
career in Iași and Bucharest. He moved to France in 1923, where he
wrote poetry, plays and philosophy, and also worked in cinema. In
1944 he was deported and killed in Auschwitz.

LAURA FUSCO is a poet and theatre director. Her publications include
Aqua Nuda (2011), *Da Da Da* (2012), *La pesatrice di perle* (2015) and
Limbo (2018). She lives in Turin.

JAMES GARZA is currently finishing his PhD in Translation Studies at
the University of Leeds. His translation of Itō Shizuo's 'Going Home'
won the 2019 Stephen Spender Prize.

REBECCA RUTH GOULD is the author of *Cityscapes* (2019) and
Writers and Rebels (2016), and a translator from Persian, Georgian,
and Russian. She is Professor, Islamic World and Comparative
Literature, at the University of Birmingham.

DURS GRÜNBEIN was born in Dresden in 1962, and now lives in
Berlin and Rome. Since 2005 he has been Professor for Poetics and
Aesthetics at the Kunstakademie Düsseldorf. His poetry has been
translated into several languages.

VOLHA HAPEYEVA is a Belarusian poet, translator and linguist with
eight books to her name. Her work is translated into a number of
languages and she has held residency scholarships in Austria,
Latvia, Germany and Switzerland. She collaborates with electronic
musicians on audiovisual performances.

BRIAN HENRY has translated Aleš Šteger's *The Book of Things* and *Above
the Sky Beneath the Earth*, Tomaž Šalamun's *Woods and Chalices*, and
Aleš Debeljak's *Smugglers*, among other books.

TOSHIKO HIRATA is one of the most notable contemporary Japanese women poets. She has published more than ten collections of poetry, as well as novels, plays and essays.

ANDREW HOUWEN is a translator of Dutch and Japanese poetry. He translated, with Chikako Nihei, the post-war Japanese poet Tarō Naka's *Music: Selected Poems* (Isobar Press, 2018). Together with Nihei, he has also had translations of tanka by Kunio Tsukamoto published in *Modern Poetry in Translation*.

ERIC E. HYETT is a poet, writer and translator from Brookline, MA. Eric's poetry appears in magazines and journals, recently *The Worcester Review, Cincinnati Review, The Hudson Review, Harvard Review Online*.

NORIKO IBARAGI (1926–2006) was a leading poet associated with the magazine *Kai* (Oar), who came to prominence during the 1950s. She published nine volumes of poetry, various collections of essays, and an anthology of Korean poetry in her own translations. Her most famous poem, 'When I Was at My Most Beautiful', was set to music by Pete Seeger.

ITSUKO ISHIKAWA (b.1933) is a committed anti-war and anti-nuclear activist poet. The experiences of her childhood have contributed to her extensive poetry and prose writings on war, imperialism and authoritarianism.

RINA KIKUCHI is a professor at Shiga University and a visiting fellow at the University of Canberra. Her research focuses on modern and contemporary Japanese women's poetry, including translating their works into English.

SHLOMO LAUFER is a prolific Hebrew poet and novelist, editor and translator. Born in war-torn Lvov in 1940, Laufer arrived in Israel with his family after a childhood of wandering.

KAREN LEEDER is a writer, translator and academic, and teaches German at New College, Oxford, where she runs the project Mediating Modern Poetry. Her translations of Durs Grünbein were awarded the Stephen Spender Prize (2011) and the John Frederick Nims Memorial Prize (2018). *Porcelain: Poem on the Downfall of my City* will be published by Seagull Books in Autumn 2020.

CAROLINE MALDONADO's publications include: *Your Call Keeps us Awake*, a co-translation from Italian with Allen Prowle of poems by Rocco Scotellaro, *Isabella* (Smokestack Books) and *What they Say in Avenale* (IDP 2014).

STEPH MORRIS' translation of Brigitte Reimann's diaries, *It all tastes of farewell* is forthcoming from Seagull Books. His poetry has appeared in *Rialto*, *Ink Sweat & Tears* and various gardens.

ERÍN MOURE is one of Canada's most respected poets, as well as a translator from French, Galician, Portuguese, and Spanish. She has translated several volumes of Chus Pato's poetry into English, including *At the Limit* (2018).

CHŪYA NAKAHARA (1907–1937) was a modernist poet and translator from French. Despite his early death, his works are now classics of modern literature.

SAWAKO NAKAYASU's new, forthcoming books are *Pink Waves* (Omnidawn) and *Some Girls Walk Into The Country They Are From* (Wave Books). She teaches at Brown University.

KATSUMASA NISHIHARA has translated Pound, Williams, Stevens and many other poets. He and Elliott have worked as co-translators and have completed, among others, half-a-dozen Tanikawa volumes.

KEI OKAMOTO was born in 1983 and began writing poetry in his late twenties. His first collection, *Graffiti*, was awarded the Nakahara Chuya Prize and the Mr. H Prize in 2015. His second collection, *Zekkei Note*, about his travels in Southeast Asia and Japan, won the Hagiwara Sakutaro Prize.

SAYAKA OSAKI (1982–) often represents Japan at international literary festivals. Her second collection of poetry, *Pointing Impossible* (Seidosha, 2014), won the Nakahara Chūya Prize. Her most recent collection is *New Habitat* (Seidosha, 2018).

TAKUJI ŌTE (1887–1934) was a pioneering Japanese symbolist and one of the first Japanese poets to translate Baudelaire directly from the French. His work explored the synaesthetic potential of words.

CHUS PATO is one of the major Galician poets writing today.

RAYMOND QUENEAU (1903–1976) was a French novelist, poet, songwriter, critic, editor and co-founder and president of Oulipo. His books include *Zazie in the Métro*, *A Hundred Thousand Billion Poems* and *Elementary Morality*.

PETER ROBINSON is a poet and translator who has been awarded the Cheltenham Prize, the John Florio Prize, and two PBS Recommendations. His versions of Noriko Ibaragi, with Fumiko Horikawa, were published as *When I Was at My Most Beautiful and Other Poems* (Skate Press, 1992). An enlarged selection, in collaboration with Andrew Houwen, is forthcoming.

BETSY ROSENBERG's book of poems *A Future More Vivid* was published by Sheep Meadow Press in 2014 and appeared in Shlomo Laufer's Hebrew translation with Carmel Publishing House in 2018.

ANNIE RUTHERFORD works as programme co-ordinator for StAnza, Scotland's international poetry festival, and as a writer and translator. Her translation of German poet Nora Gomringer, *Hydra's Heads*, is available from Burning Eye Books.

AXEL SCHULZE (1943–2004) lived in the GDR throughout its existence, where he published several poetry collections, a children's book, and appeared in many significant anthologies and magazines.

MOTOYUKI SHIBATA has translated American authors both contemporary and classic, including Paul Auster, Kelly Link, and Mark Twain. He edits MONKEY, a tri-annual Japanese-language literary journal based in Tokyo.

YOSHINO SHIGIHARA is a London-based Japanese artist and musician. She often improvises hand drawings and constructs them afterwards. She plays music as 'Yama Warashi' and been creating artwork, costume and comic books for the project.

TARA SKURTU is a two-time U.S. Fulbright grantee and recipient of two Academy of American Poets prizes, a Marcia Keach Poetry Prize, and a Robert Pinsky Global Fellowship. She is the author of *The Amoeba Game*.

ALEŠ ŠTEGER has published seven books of poetry, three novels, and two books of essays in Slovenian. His books in English include *The Book of Things*, *Berlin*, *Essential Baggage*, *Above the Sky Beneath the Earth*, and the novel *Absolution*.

KAYVAN TAHMASEBIAN is a translator, literary critic and author of the poetry collection *Lecture on Fear and Other Poems* (Radical Paper Press, 2019). He is co-translator of *High Tide of the Eyes: Poems by Bijan Elahi* (The Operating System, 2019).

SHUZO TAKIGUCHI (1903–1979), poet, painter, and art critic, was one of the most prominent Surrealists in Japan.

YUKI TANAKA holds an MFA in poetry from the Michener Centre for Writers, and a Ph.D. in English from Washington University in St. Louis. He teaches at Hosei University, Japan.

SHUNTARO TANIKAWA, at 88, has remained since 1952 modern Japan's most well-known living poet in Japanese, English and some other languages. He is a proverbial household name.

YEMISRACH TASSEW is a poetry-loving commercial lawyer working in Trade and Investment Advisory services in Ethiopia.

MISRAK TEREFE is a young poet and performer based in Addis Ababa. She is a founding member of the Tobiya Poetic Jazz group. She was the first female poet to put out her own VCD and is featured on the Tobiya DVD (vol 1). She has published one collection, *Chew Berenda* (Salt Market).

PHILIP TERRY was born in Belfast, and is a poet, translator, and a writer of fiction. He is currently translating Ice Age signs from the caves at Lascaux and edited *The Penguin Book of Oulipo* (2019).

SPENCER THURLOW is the current Poet Laureate of West Tisbury, Massachusetts. His poetry or translations have appeared in *World Literature Today, Cincinnati Review, The Comstock Review*, and others.

LYNN XU was born in Shanghai. She is the author of *Debts & Lessons* and a chapbook, *June*. She teaches at Columbia University.

KYOKO YOSHIDA's stories have appeared *BooksActually's Gold Standard, After Coetzee*, and others. Her books include the fiction collection *Disorientalism*. She has translated Masataka Matsuda, Kiwao Nomura, Shu Matsui among others

SARAH-JEAN ZUBAIR is a postgraduate student in English literature at University College London. She holds an MA in English and Comparative Literature from Columbia University, New York.